Envision It! | Handbook

Reading STREET

Grade 3

PEARSON

Glenview, Illinois • Boston, M
Chandler, Arizona • Upper Sad

ISBN-13: 978-0-328-58086-6
ISBN-10:   0-328-58086-4
6 7 8 9 10 V056 18 17 16 15 14 13
CC1

Envision It! | Handbook

A note to you!

The *Envision It! Handbook* will help you learn more about comprehension strategies, comprehension skills, vocabulary, and genres. You can use it on your own, with a partner, or with your teacher. Take a look inside and you will find lessons, illustrations, photographs, and charts that will help you become a better reader!

A note to your teacher. . .

The *Envision It! Handbook* will help your students learn more about comprehension strategies, comprehension skills, vocabulary, and genres. You can use it in small groups to enhance your reading instruction, or students can use it on their own or with a partner to guide their reading.

The *Envision It! Handbook* is filled with lessons, illustrations, photographs, and charts that will help your students become better readers!

Envision It! | Handbook

Contents

Let's Think About Strategies

Let's Think About Skills

Comprehension Skills (continued)

Let's Think About Vocabulary

Let's Think About Genre

Envision It! | Visual Strategies

Background Knowledge
Important Ideas
Inferring
Monitor and Clarify
Predict and Set Purpose
Questioning
Story Structure
Summarize
Text Structure
Visualize

Comprehension Strategies

As you read,

- try to make sense of what you are reading by thinking about what you know.
- notice when you don't understand something.

Comprehension strategies are ways to think about reading in order to better understand what you read.

Ready to Try It?

Background Knowledge

Background knowledge is what you already know about a topic based on your reading and personal experience. Make connections to people, places, and things. Use background knowledge before, during, and after reading to monitor and adjust comprehension.

To use background knowledge
- with fiction, preview the title, author's name, and illustrations
- with nonfiction, preview chapter titles, headings, and other text features
- think about what you already know

This reminds me of a book I read.

Let's **Think** About **Reading!**

When I use background knowledge, I ask myself
- Does this character remind me of someone?
- How is this story or text similar to others I have read?
- What else do I know about this topic?

Background Knowledge
When Charlie McButton Lost Power
by Suzanne Collins

We all have background knowledge. That's what we already know. What I know about storms and younger brothers helped me understand Charlie's feelings when I read When Charlie McButton Lost Power.

He was upset. Lightning hit an electrical tower and knocked out power at his house. He couldn't play computer games or watch television. I feel like that when the power at our house goes out during storms.

Also, I have a little brother. Sometimes he annoys me, but mostly we get along. We like to play together like Charlie and Isabel Jane do.

Important Ideas

Important ideas are essential facts in a nonfiction selection. Important ideas provide clues to the author's purpose.

To identify important ideas

- read all titles, headings, and captions
- look for words in italics, bold print, or bulleted lists
- look for signal words such as *for example* and *most important*
- use photos, illustrations, or diagrams
- note how the text is organized— cause and effect, question and answer, or other ways

The caption under the photograph gives more information about wolves.

Let's Think About Reading!

When I identify important ideas, I ask myself

- What information is included in bold or italics?
- Are there signal words and phrases?
- What do illustrations, photos, diagrams, and charts show?
- How is the text organized?

Important Ideas
How Do You Raise a Raisin?
by Pam Muñoz Ryan

When I read How Do You Raise a Raisin?, I looked for facts that would answer the question. Those facts are the important ideas.

The author wrote questions in poems, and then she wrote the answers after the poems. That's where I looked for the important ideas.

This is what I learned.
- Raisins are dried grapes.
- You need hot weather, a dry climate, and plenty of water to grow grapes.
- Grapes for raisins grow on grapevines.
- Grapes are dried in the sun for 2-3 weeks to turn into raisins.
- It takes 4 pounds of grapes to make one pound of raisins.
- Raisins are good for you!

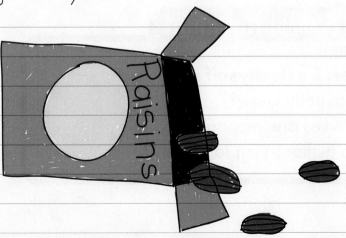

Inferring

When we **infer** we use background knowledge with clues in the text to come up with our own ideas about what the author is trying to present.

To infer

- identify what you already know
- combine what you know with text clues to come up with ideas

Let's Think About Reading!

When I infer, I ask myself
- What do I already know?
- Which text clues are important?
- What is the author trying to present?

Inferring
I Love Saturdays y domingos
by Alma Flor Ada

An inference is a conclusion or idea that I figure out for myself when I'm reading something.

   In I Love Saturdays y domingos, there are foreign words that I didn't understand. I inferred that the girl in the story knows two languages. Then I read that one of her grandfathers came from Mexico. I inferred that the language that I couldn't read is Spanish. I was also able to infer what these words meant because the author gave clues in the text!

   I also inferred that the girl in the story is loved by all of her grandparents. They show it in different ways and with different words.

Monitor and Clarify

We **monitor** comprehension to make sure our reading makes sense. When we don't understand, we **clarify**, to adjust comprehension.

To monitor and clarify
- use background knowledge as you read
- reread, ask questions, or use illustrations

This doesn't make sense! I'll slow down and reread.

Let's **Think** About **Reading!**

When I monitor and clarify, I ask myself
- Do I understand what I'm reading?
- What doesn't make sense?
- What strategies can I try here?

Monitor and Clarify
Penguin Chick
by Betty Tatham

When I monitor my reading, I ask myself if what I read makes sense. If it doesn't, I need to clarify. That means figuring out what I don't understand.

There were words I didn't understand in Penguin Chick. One was "krill." I reread the sentence it was in and figured out that krill are tiny shrimplike creatures. Then I looked at the illustration of a krill on the bottom of the page. That helped me a lot!

Then I realized that whenever the author uses a hard or new word, she puts it in italics. Then she explains what the word means before or after it. When I didn't understand what "crèche" meant, I kept reading. I learned that a crèche is a penguin nursery.

I learned a lot about penguins in this article! They're my new favorite animal!

Predict and Set Purpose

We **predict** to tell what might happen next in a story. We **set a purpose** to guide our reading.

To predict and set a purpose
- preview the title, author's name, and illustrations or photos
- identify why you're reading
- use what you already know
- check your predictions

Let's **Think** About **Reading!**

When I predict and set a purpose, I ask myself
- What do I already know?
- What do I think will probably happen?
- What is my purpose for reading?

Predict and Set Purpose
Tops and Bottoms
adapted by Janet Stevens

Before I read Tops and Bottoms, I looked at the illustrations. They were so funny! My purpose in reading was to enjoy a funny story.

After I read the first two pages, I predicted that Hare would trick Bear somehow. I was right. Hare planted only crops that grew below ground because he got "bottoms."

When Bear got angry and wanted "bottoms" for the next crop, I predicted that Hare would trick Bear again. I was right. Hare planted only crops that grew above ground.

My third prediction was wrong. I predicted that Bear would finally get some of the crops since he wanted tops and bottoms. I was surprised when Hare planted corn. He gave Bear the roots and tassels and kept the middle (the corn) for himself!

Questioning

Questioning is asking good questions about information in text. Ask questions before, during, and after reading.

To question
- read with a question in mind
- stop, think, and record your questions
- check your understanding

Let's Think About Reading!

When I question, I ask myself
- Have I asked a good question with a question word?
- What questions help me make sense of my reading?
- What does the author mean?

Questioning
The Story of the Statue of Liberty
by Betsy and Giulio Maestro

Before I read The Story of the Statue of Liberty, I looked at the pictures. I wondered about some things. I thought of these questions.

- Who made the Statue of Liberty?
- Why was it made?
- Why was there a small statue in one of the pictures?
- Why was there a picture of just the head of the statue?
- Why was the statue taken apart?

As I read, I found the answers to most of my questions.

I didn't understand one thing, though. Why did they build it in Paris and then take it apart and rebuild it in New York? Why didn't they just build it in New York in the first place?

Story Structure

Story structure is the order of a story from beginning to end. Use this information to summarize, or retell, the plot.

To identify story structure
- note events at the beginning, middle, and end of the story
- use this information to summarize, or retell, the story

Let's Think About Reading!

When I identify story structure, I ask myself
- What happens in the beginning, middle, and end?
- How can I use this information to summarize?
- How might this affect future events?

Story Structure
My Rows and Piles of Coins
by Tololwa M. Mollel

Story structure is how a story is arranged. It's what happens in the beginning, middle, and end of a story.

My Rows and Piles of Coins is about a boy named Saruni.

BEGINNING—Saruni wants to save his money to buy a bicycle.

MIDDLE—Saruni works hard to save up for the bike.

END—The surprise ending is that his father buys a motorbike for himself and gives Saruni his old bike!

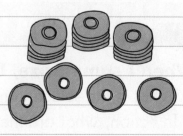

Summarize

We **summarize**, or retell, to check our understanding of what we've read. A summary is no more than a few sentences.

To summarize fiction
- tell what happens in the story
- include the characters' goals, how they try to reach them, and if they are successful

To summarize nonfiction
- tell the main idea
- think about how the selection is organized

...and that's how Lewis and Clark helped create new communities.

Let's Think About Reading!

When I summarize, I ask myself
- What is the selection mainly about?
- In fiction, what are the characters' goals?
- In nonfiction, how is this information organized?

Summarize
The Man Who Invented Basketball
by Edwin Brit Wyckoff

The Man Who Invented Basketball is a biography of James Naismith. When I summarize what I've read, I only tell the most important things. This is my summary.

When James Naismith was young, his parents, grandmother, and brother all died. This made James want to help people. He became a minister. He thought he could help young men be better people through sports. When he was teaching at a YMCA training school, he thought up the game of basketball so that the men would have a fun inside game for the wintertime. This is how basketball was invented.

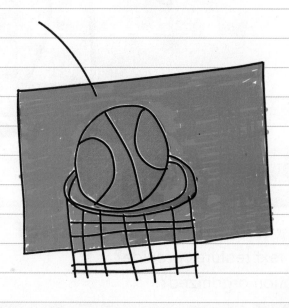

Text Structure

We use **text structure** to look for how the author has organized the text; for example, cause and effect, problem and solution, sequence, or compare and contrast.

To identify text structure
- before reading: preview text features
- during reading: notice the organization
- after reading: recall the organization and summarize

This article uses sequence to explain how soil is formed.

SOIL HOW IT'S FORMED

Let's Think About Reading!

When I identify text structure, I ask myself
- What clues do text features provide?
- How is information organized?

Text Structure
Amazing Bird Nests
by Ron Fridell

Text structure is how an article is organized.

    I previewed <u>Amazing Bird Nests</u> by looking at the photographs and reading the heads and captions.

    The author uses different structures within a section of the aritcle. One of the parts, "Very Small and Very Big," uses a compare-contrast structure. It compares a hummingbird's nest to an eagle's nest.

    In another part, "Watch Them Grow," the author uses sequence to organize facts and details about how birds build nests, lay eggs, and care for chicks.

Visualize

We **visualize** by forming pictures in our minds about what is happening.

To visualize
- combine what you already know with words and phrases from the text
- use your senses to put yourself in the text

Let's Think About Reading!

When I visualize, I ask myself
- Which words and phrases help me form pictures?
- How can my senses put me in the story?

Visualize
Suki's Kimono
by Chieri Uegaki

Visualizing means making pictures in your mind.

When I read Suki's Kimono, I used the author's words to picture what Suki looks like and what she's doing. I could picture Suki clip-clopping her way to school in her blue kimono. It has a pattern of fans on it. Her obi, or sash, is golden yellow. Her clip-cloppy shoes, called geta, are red. I could picture her butterfly sleeves blowing in the wind when she raises her arms.

Sometimes the characters in a story visualize too. Wearing her kimono helps Suki visualize the good time she had with her grandma at a street festival.

Visualizing helps me understand stories better!

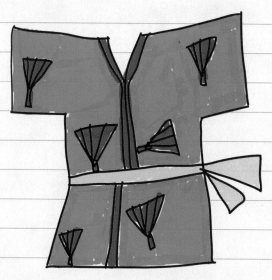

Envision It! | Visual Skills

Author's Purpose

Cause and Effect

Compare and Contrast

Draw Conclusions

Fact and Opinion

Generalize

Main Idea and Details

Graphic Sources

Literary Elements

Sequence

Classify and Categorize

Steps in a Process

Comprehension Skills

As you read,
- pay attention to the way the text is organized.
- think about the topic of the text.
- compare what you are reading with other things you have read.
- think like an author. What is the author's purpose for writing?

Comprehension skills are routines you use automatically in order to better understand what you read.

Ready to **Try** It? ▶

Author's Purpose

To Persuade

To Inform

To Entertain

An author's purpose is the reason an author has for writing.

To Express Emotion

How to Find Author's Purpose

Is the author writing to persuade, to inform, to entertain, or to express ideas and feelings?

See It!

- Before you read, look at the photographs or illustrations. What do you see? How do the images make you feel? Why do you think the author chose those images?

- Are there a lot of subheads, text boxes, or other graphics in the selection? Is the text bright and colorful? Does this give you an idea about the author's purpose?

Say It!

- Take turns reading aloud and listening to the first few paragraphs of a text with a partner. Predict the author's purpose. Then discuss the kinds of words the author uses. Are the author's words persuasive, entertaining, informative, or expressive?

Do It!

- Write the author's main ideas. What is the author trying to say?

- Draw an image of one of the author's main ideas, or make a graphic organizer like the one below.

Objectives

● Ask questions, clear up anything you don't understand, and look for facts and details. Support your answers with details from the text. ● Tell in order the main events of a story. Explain how they will affect future events in a story.

Envision It! | Skill Strategy

Skill

Strategy

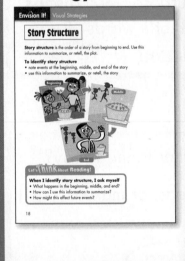

READING STREET ONLINE
ENVISION IT! ANIMATIONS
www.ReadingStreet.com

Comprehension Skill

🎯 Author's Purpose

- The author's purpose is the reason an author has for writing.

- An author writes to inform, to persuade, to entertain, or to express an opinion.

- Use what you learned about author's purpose and the graphic organizer below as you read "Saturday Is Market Day." Then write a paragraph explaining how the text would change if the author's purpose were different.

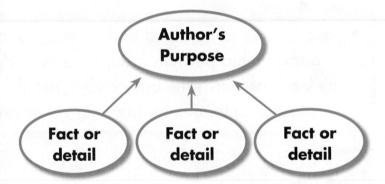

Comprehension Strategy

🎯 Story Structure

As you read, think about the events that happen at the beginning, middle, and end of the story. Using the structure of a story can help you retell the story in your own words and improve your comprehension.

Saturday Is Market Day

My family lives in a little village in Africa. Every Saturday we go to town to sell our head scarves. Mama makes the scarves. Sometimes I help. They are the very best scarves you can buy.

Papa pulled the cart into the market as the sun came up. My sister Fusi and I laid out the scarves. It was not long before customers stopped by to look. A woman and her daughter bought two. Soon we began to sell many more.

At ten, drummers set up near us. As they played, Papa and Fusi danced. Mama and I clapped along.

Later, one customer had me turn around and around. She was looking at the scarf I was wearing that I made myself. She bought my scarf! It was a good market day. I am looking forward to next Saturday.

Skill What is the author's purpose for writing this story? What facts and details help you to know?

Strategy What happens in the beginning, middle, and end of this story?

Your Turn!

Need a Review? See the *Envision It!* Skills and Strategies for additional help.

Ready to Try It? As you read other text, use what you've learned about author's purpose and story structure to help you understand it.

Objectives
- Use ideas you get from different parts of a text to make predictions.
- Set a purpose for reading a text.
- Monitor your comprehension of a text and adjust your reading based on how well you understand what you are reading.

Envision It! Skill Strategy

Skill

Strategy

Comprehension Skill

🎯 Author's Purpose

- The author's purpose is the reason an author writes something.

- There are many reasons for writing: to persuade, to inform, to entertain, or to express ideas and feelings.

- Use what you learned about an author's purpose and the graphic organizer below as you read "Salsa Garden."

Before You Read Read the title. For which reasons might the author write a piece with this title?

As You Read Think about the author's purpose.

After You Read Now what do you think the author's purpose was? Why?

Comprehension Strategy

🎯 Predict and Set Purpose

Before you read, set a purpose for why you are reading the text. What outcome, or result, do you want from reading? Then use ideas to predict what will happen and why. What do you think the story will be about? As you read, check your predictions and make new ones.

Salsa Garden

David saw the sign his father put on the garden fence. It said Salsa Garden.

"Salsa?" David read aloud. "Can you grow salsa?"

Dad replied, "Just watch and see what comes up."

Each time David helped by watering and pulling weeds, he looked at the green plants. They all looked different. Not one looked like salsa.

Finally, harvest time came. First, Dad dug in the ground and pulled out round white things that looked a lot like onions. Then, he pulled off pods hanging from a plant. They looked a lot like hot peppers. Next, he cut a green leafy plant that smelled spicy. Finally, Dad pulled round red balls from a fat vine. They sure looked a lot like tomatoes.

"Where's the salsa, Dad?" David asked as he followed his father to the kitchen.

Dad washed and cut everything up. He dumped his harvest into a machine with a sharp blade and turned it on. When he opened the lid, it was full of salsa!

Strategy Make a prediction and set a purpose before you read, using the title and photos. What do you think the story will be about? Confirm your prediction as you read.

Strategy Set a purpose before you read. What outcome do you want from reading this selection?

Skill What is the author's purpose? How do you know?

Your Turn!

Need a Review? See the *Envision It!* Skills and Strategies for additional help.

Ready to Try It? As you read other text, use what you've learned about author's purpose and predict and set purpose to help you understand it.

33

Skill

Strategy

Comprehension Skill

Author's Purpose

- Sometimes authors tell you their purposes for writing. They write to inform, entertain, persuade, or express an opinion.

- An author can write to try to persuade you to think or do something by using "loaded words," or strong words.

- Use what you learned about author's purpose and a graphic organizer like the one below as you read "New York City." Then write a paragraph explaining the author's purpose.

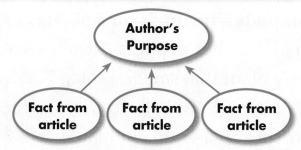

Comprehension Strategy

Background Knowledge

Good readers use what they already know to help them understand their reading. As you read, make connections to your own life. Have you ever seen or experienced what you are reading about? This will help you understand what you read.

NEW YORK CITY

I'm going to talk you into coming to New York City. It's a terrific place to visit. There are many things to see and do. New York City is the largest city in the United States.

In New York City you can visit the Empire State Building. This grand building opened in 1931. It is 102 stories tall! For many years, it was the tallest building in the world.

The Statue of Liberty is a breathtaking place! This statue stands on Bedloe's Island in New York Harbor. The Statue of Liberty rises to more than 300 feet. People come from all over the world to see this famous statue.

If you enjoy great plays and musical events, Broadway, a street in the center of New York City, has it all. It is the most famous theater district in the country. You will enjoy your visit and have a wonderful time when you come to New York!

Skill What is the author's stated purpose for writing?

Strategy What do you already know about New York City?

Strategy What do you already know about the Statue of Liberty?

Your Turn!

Need a Review? See the *Envision It!* Skills and Strategies for additional help.

Ready to Try It? As you read other text, use what you've learned about author's purpose and background knowledge to help you understand it.

35

Cause and Effect

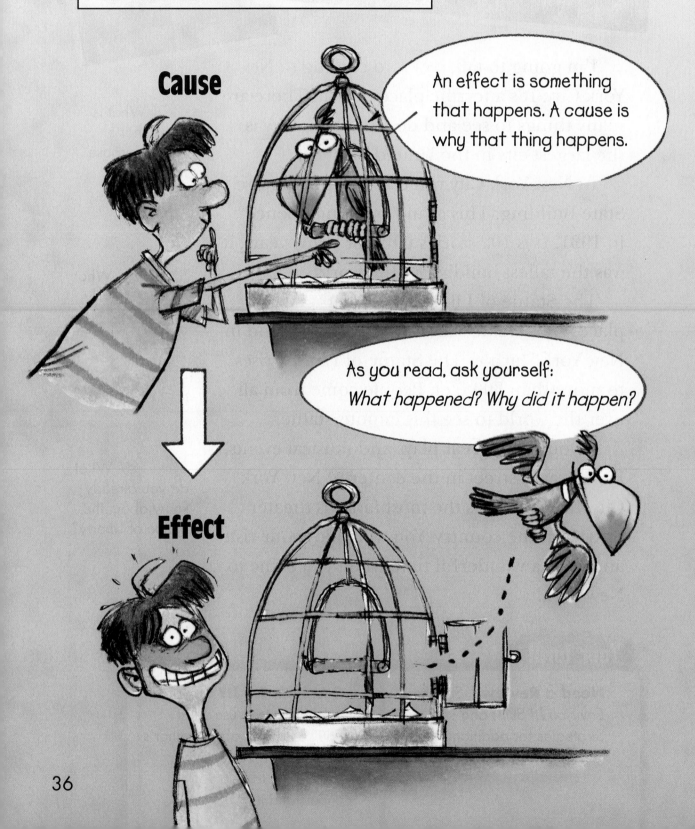

How to Identify Cause and Effect

A cause tells why something happened. An effect is what happened.

See It!

- Look for clue words in a text, such as *because, so, since,* and *for that reason.* They tell about cause and effect.

- Make a picture in your mind as you read the following sentence: *Matt opened the window. The wind blew his pile of papers to the floor.* Identify the cause by asking, "What did Matt do?" Identify the effect by asking, "What happened after he did this?"

Say It!

- To understand cause and effect, ask yourself or a partner "What happened?" and "Why did this happen?"

- Listen to a partner read sentences or paragraphs aloud. Listen for clue words, such as *because* or *so,* that tell about cause and effect.

Do It!

- Write an effect to the following cause: *It started to rain when we were at the park.*

- Make a graphic organizer that helps you figure out cause and effect. A cause can have more than one effect.

- Write "what" and "why" questions about a text to a partner. Have your partner answer aloud or in writing.

Objectives
- Identify the cause and effect relationships among ideas in the text.

Envision It! | Skill Strategy

Skill

Strategy

Comprehension Skill

🎯 Cause and Effect

- A cause tells why something happened.

- An effect is what happened.

- Words such as *because* and *so* are clues that can help you figure out a cause and its effects.

- Use what you learned about cause and effect and the graphic organizer below as you read "Winter Blooms." Then write a paragraph that explains why you have to keep plants indoors to grow in the winter.

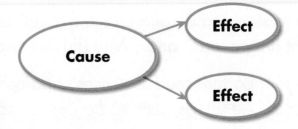

Comprehension Strategy

🎯 Predict and Set Purpose

When you read, it is important to think about why you are reading. Ask yourself what it is you want to find out. Make predictions about what you think will happen. Stop and check to see if your predictions are correct.

Winter Blooms

Have you ever wanted to grow plants in the winter? During winter months, the Earth tilts away from sun, so there is less sunlight and less heat. Plants need sunlight in order to grow.

But wait! You can still grow plants inside, even during the coldest days of the year. Place your plants in front of a window that faces south or west because they will get more direct light. You can tell if a plant is not getting enough light by how it grows. If a plant leans toward a window, it wants more sunlight!

Plants are like people. They also need water. If the leaves on your plants begin to shrivel up or fall off, it is because you aren't giving them enough water. But be careful, you can also over water plants.

If you learn the secrets to growing indoor plants, you too can have winter blooms.

Skill Which clue word in this paragraph shows a cause-and-effect relationship?

Skill What is the cause of a plant that leans toward a window?

Strategy Predict what reasons the author will give to explain why plants are like people.

Your Turn!

Need a Review? See the *Envision It!* Skills and Strategies for additional help.

Ready to Try It? As you read other text, use what you've learned about cause and effect and predict and set purpose to help you understand it.

Skill

Strategy

Comprehension Skill

Cause and Effect

• A cause tells why something happened.

• An effect is what happened.

• *Because* and *so* are clue words that show a cause-and-effect relationship.

• Use what you learned about cause and effect and a graphic organizer like the one below to read "Birds of Prey." Then use your graphic organizer to write a paragraph that explains the cause-and-effect relationship.

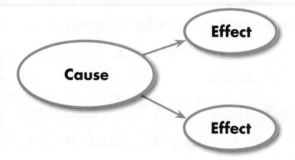

Comprehension Strategy

Monitor and Clarify

Good readers think about what they are reading. They stop reading when they are confused and try to figure out what's wrong. When you are confused, go back and reread to help clarify your understanding.

Birds of Prey

Eagles are large birds of prey that are members of the falcon family. Like all birds of prey, eagles have very large hooked beaks, strong legs, and powerful talons or claws. Another advantage that eagles have is their keen eyesight. Eagles can spot their prey from very long distances because they have large pupils.

Eagles are different from many other birds of prey. They are larger, have a more powerful build, and have heavier heads and bills. Most eagles are larger than any other birds of prey apart from vultures.

Eagles build their nests in tall trees or on high cliffs so that their young chicks are protected from other animals. In recent years, eagles have fallen prey to their environment. Many eagles have moved away from the heavily populated areas in the United States or disappeared entirely because of human expansion.

Skill What clue word is in this paragraph? What cause and effect does it show?

Strategy Are you having trouble understanding how eagles are different from other birds of prey? Go back and reread this paragraph aloud.

Your Turn!

Need a Review? See the *Envision It!* Skills and Strategies for additional help.

Ready to Try It? As you read other text, use what you've learned about cause and effect and monitoring and clarifying to help you understand it.

Envision It! Skill Strategy

Skill

Strategy

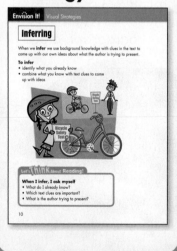

Comprehension Skill

Cause and Effect

• An effect is something that happens.

• A cause is why that thing happens.

• An effect may have more than one cause.

• Use what you learned about cause and effect and a chart like the one below as you read "A New Life." Then write a short paragraph summarizing the cause-and-effect relationships.

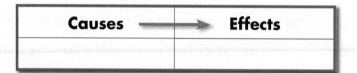

Causes ⟶	Effects

Comprehension Strategy

Inferring

As you read a selection, you make inferences, or decisions that make sense after you combine the details or facts the author has included with what you already know. When you come up with your own ideas based on information in a text, you are inferring.

A New Life

An *immigrant* is a person who has moved from one country into another. According to the U.S. Census Bureau, in 1990, the foreign-born population in the United States was about 19.8 million. By the year 2000, that number had grown to 37.2 million! Immigrants make up about 12.5 percent of the United States population.

There are many reasons that people have immigrated to the United States. Many people view the United States as a place where people can achieve any goal if they put their minds to it and work hard. Some come here because of the opportunities to build better lives for themselves and their families. Some move here so they can experience the freedom that the United States offers.

Immigrants bring with them their cultural heritage, traditions, and new ideas. They have helped build the United States to make it what it is today.

Skill What has caused some people to move to the United States?

Strategy What are some of the benefits of people immigrating to the United States?

Your Turn!

Need a Review? See the *Envision It! Skills and Strategies* for additional help.

Ready to Try It? As you read other text, use what you've learned about cause and effect and inferring to help you understand it.

Compare and Contrast

As you read, think about what is alike and what is different.

Alike

Different

How to Compare and Contrast

When we compare and contrast things, we say what is similar and different about them. During reading, we think about what is alike and what is different.

See It!

- Look at the picture on page 44. It compares and contrasts two well-known stories. What are the stories? How are they similar? How are they different?

- Look at the illustrations that go with a story you are reading. If characters are pictured, compare and contrast them.

Say It!

- Name an item in the classroom. Have a partner tell you something that is similar to that object, and something that is different. Take turns.

Do It!

- A Venn diagram is very helpful when you want to tell how things are alike or different. Draw two circles or ovals that intersect, as shown below:

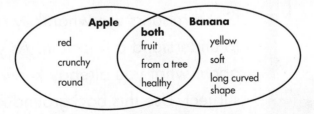

Envision It! | Skill Strategy

Skill

Strategy

Comprehension Skill

Compare and Contrast

• When you compare, you tell how two or more things are alike.

• When you contrast, you tell only how the things are different.

• Use what you learned about compare and contrast and the graphic organizer below as you read "On the Farm."

	Farm	Subdivision
David		
Marcia		
Katie		

Comprehension Strategy

Background Knowledge

Good readers use what they already know to understand a selection. As you read, think about what you already know about the subject. Use this background knowledge to help you understand and connect with what you are reading.

On the Farm

The Marshall family lives on a big farm. It has eight hundred acres. An acre is about as big as a football field. There are three children in the family. David is twelve and Marcia is ten. Their little sister, Katie, is eight years old. In the spring their family plants seeds. They plant potatoes, sweet corn, and other vegetables. The children all help with the work.

Many new subdivisions have been built around the farm. David thinks all the houses look all the same. Marcia feels sorry for the families in those houses. She knows the children do not have much room to run around.

Sometimes Katie thinks about what it would be like to live in a big neighborhood. She thinks that she would like to have lots of playmates.

David and Marcia both want to be farmers someday. Katie thinks she would like to try something different.

Strategy As you read, think about your background knowledge. What do you know about life on a farm and life in a subdivision?

Skill Compare and contrast how David, Marcia, and Katie each feel about living on the farm.

Your Turn!

⏸ **Need a Review?** See the *Envision It!* Skills and Strategies for additional help.

▶ **Ready to Try It?** As you read other text, use what you've learned about compare and contrast and background knowledge to help you understand it.

Objectives

• Identify words that paint a picture in your mind and appeal to your senses. • Monitor your comprehension of a text and adjust your reading based on how well you understand what you are reading.

Envision It! | Skill Strategy

Skill

Strategy

READING STREET ONLINE
ENVISION IT! ANIMATIONS
www.ReadingStreet.com

Comprehension Skill

🎯 Compare and Contrast

• Compare by telling how two or more things are alike or different.

• Contrast by telling only how two or more things are different.

• Use what you learned about compare and contrast and the graphic organizer below as you read "Snuggles and Tippy." Use the text and the graphic organizer to write a short paragraph that compares and contrasts Snuggles and Tippy.

Snuggles	Tippy

Comprehension Strategy

🎯 Visualize

As you read, picture in your mind the characters, the setting, and the events of the story. Use the details that tell you how something looks, sounds, tastes, feels, or smells to help form images. If you are unable to visualize what you are reading, stop and reread until you can picture it.

Snuggles and Tippy

Rita had a small black cat named Snuggles. The cat had bright green eyes. Her neighbor Joe had a big black dog he called Tippy. Tippy had a white spot on the tip of his tail.

Joe was busy playing catch with his dog when Rita walked out into the backyard. "Where is your cat?" asked Joe. "Does she play outside? Tippy loves to be with people."

"Cats are much more particular," replied Rita. "They will not play with just anyone."

Just then Snuggles walked out of the house. Tippy barked and Snuggles ran. She was so frightened that she climbed right up into the branches of the nearest tree.

"Well," said Joe, "that is another difference between cats and dogs. My dog would never run up a tree."

Snuggles hissed at Tippy from the safety of her branch. Rita was upset. "Well, my cat would never scare your dog!"

"I am not sure about that," laughed Joe, as he rescued the angry cat.

Strategy Here's a good place to stop and visualize the pets in the story. What details help you picture them?

Skill Compare and contrast how Joe and Rita feel about their pets. What details tell you this?

Your Turn!

Need a Review? See the *Envision It!* Skills and Strategies for additional help.

Ready to Try It? As you read other text, use what you've learned about compare and contrast and visualizing to help you understand it.

Envision It! | **Skill Strategy**

Skill

Strategy

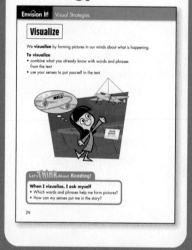

Comprehension Skill

Compare and Contrast

- When you compare and contrast two or more things, you tell how they are alike and different.

- Clue words such as *like, both, also, but, however,* and *instead of* show comparisons and contrasts.

- Use what you learned about compare and contrast and the graphic organizer below as you read "The Boxed Lunch." Then write a short paragraph comparing the two lunches.

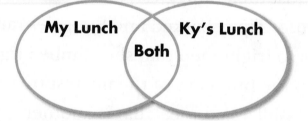

Comprehension Strategy

Visualize

While reading, look for words that help you form pictures in your mind. Forming pictures about what is happening in the story can help you enjoy and remember a story. Forming pictures in your mind can help you monitor and adjust or correct your comprehension as you read.

THE BOXED LUNCH

Ky was nervous about his first day in his new school. In Japan, Ky always brought his lunch in a bento box, which was carefully packed with eye-catching foods. Ky loved the sausage that looked like a tiny octopus. Instead of carrot sticks, he had hard-boiled eggs that looked like baby chicks just hatching. And instead of tortilla chips, he had a rice ball covered with pieces of dried seaweed so that it looked like a soccer ball.

At lunchtime, Ky's classmates began eating their lunches. Ky opened his box slowly, not sure of what his new friends would think. But they were very interested. He explained each item and showed them how to eat with chopsticks. Some boys asked to try the chopsticks. Ky promised to bring some for everyone the next day. One friend said, "I wonder how they'll work with peanut butter and jelly sandwiches."

Skill Note the clue words—*instead of*. What things are being compared? How are they the same or different?

Strategy Form a picture in your mind of a friend trying to eat a peanut butter and jelly sandwich with chopsticks. What do you see?

Your Turn!

Need a Review? See the *Envision It!* Skills and Strategies for additional help.

Ready to Try It? As you read other text, use what you've learned about compare and contrast and visualizing to help you understand it.

Draw Conclusions

Combine what you already know with new information to draw conclusions.

What I know:

Riding uphill can make you tired. Sometimes your face scrunches up when you work hard. Exercise can make you feel warm.

Conclusion:

The girl is becoming hot and tired.

How to Draw Conclusions

When we draw conclusions, we form an opinion by combining the facts and details we've been given with what we already know.

See It!

- Look at the picture on page 52. What conclusion can you make about the part of the hill that the girl has already biked up? Why?

- Picture in your mind someone who is excited, mad, or sad. What clues do they give you about their mood?

Say It!

- Talk through the conclusions you make with a partner as you read. Look back over details from the reading and use what you know from your own life. Ask your partner, "Does this conclusion make sense?"

- Take turns sharing with a small group what you already know about the topic of a text. This information can help you draw conclusions.

Do It!

- Make a graphic organizer like this one to help you draw conclusions based on facts and details.

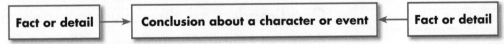

Fact or detail → Conclusion about a character or event ← Fact or detail

- Write a brief mystery where a character has to draw a conclusion based on clues. Include facts and details that help the character solve the mystery.

- Tell your partner three facts about something, and ask him or her to figure out what you are describing based on the information.

Objectives

● Examine and make judgments from the facts in the article, and support your conclusions with evidence.

Envision It! Skill Strategy

Skill

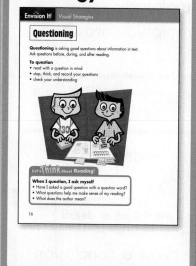

Strategy

READING STREET ONLINE
ENVISION IT! ANIMATIONS
www.ReadingStreet.com

Comprehension Skill

Draw Conclusions

• A conclusion is a decision or opinion that makes sense based on facts and details.

• The details and facts you read and what you already know will help you to draw conclusions about the text.

• Use what you learned about drawing conclusions and the graphic organizer below as you read "Collecting Stamps." Draw conclusions about how you can collect stamps without spending money.

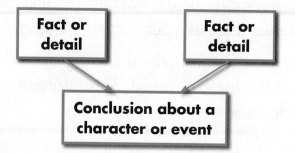

Comprehension Strategy

Questioning

Good readers ask themselves questions as they read. Literal questions, such as "Who is this character?" help you understand what you are reading. Interpretive questions, such as "Why is this happening?" and evaluative questions, such as "Do I agree with what the author is saying?" help you connect to and think about the text.

Collecting

Collecting stamps is a fun and interesting hobby. Sometimes children and young people are interested in collecting stamps. But they might not have a lot of money to buy stamps. How can you get stamps without spending money?

There are a few ways you can solve that problem. One way is to ask people to give you stamps that they don't need. Start by telling your friends and your family that you are collecting stamps. Suppose your uncle gets a letter from France. He can save the stamp and give it to you!

Strategy This is a good place to stop reading and ask a question, such as *What is the topic of this selection?*

Another way to get stamps is to trade them with other people. Once you start collecting, you might get more than one copy of the same stamp. Then you can use the copies to trade with other people for stamps that you don't have.

Skill What conclusion can you draw about why you might get more than one copy of a stamp?

Asking people to save stamps for you and trading stamps are two good ways to get stamps. Before you know it, you'll have more stamps than you can count!

Your Turn!

⏸ **Need a Review?** See the *Envision It!* Skills and Strategies for additional help.

▶ **Ready to Try It?** As you read other text, use what you've learned about drawing conclusions and questioning to help you understand it.

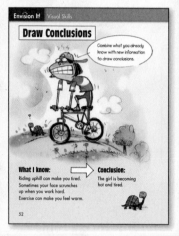

Skill

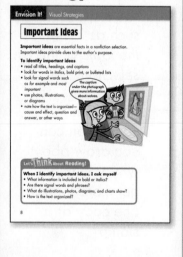

Strategy

Comprehension Skill

Draw Conclusions

- A conclusion is a decision or an opinion that makes sense based on facts and details from the text.

- Use what you already know to draw conclusions. Support your conclusions with facts and details from the text.

- Use what you learned about drawing conclusions and the graphic organizer below as you read "Before It's a Raisin, It's a Grape!" Draw a conclusion about why so many grapes are grown in California, and support your conclusion with facts and details from the text.

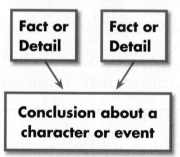

Comprehension Strategy

Important Ideas

When you are reading, look for the important ideas. These are the ideas the author explains or wants you to know. Understanding these ideas will help you understand the text as a whole.

Before It's a Raisin, It's a Grape!

Raisins come from grapes. Grapes have been grown in California for the past two hundred years. During the 1800s, men came looking for gold. Some of them ended up growing grapes instead.

Today most of the grapes we eat come from California. About 550 farmers grow grapes there. The warm, dry California weather helps grow sweet fruit.

Skill What conclusion can you draw about the decision to grow grapes in California? Support your conclusion with details and facts from the text.

Americans eat an average of eight pounds of grapes a year. People in many other countries enjoy grapes grown in the United States. People in Canada, Mexico, China, Taiwan, and Central American countries eat grapes grown in our country.

Strategy What important facts have you learned so far about grapes?

People in ancient China drank juice made from grapes mixed with snakes and frogs to feel better when they were sick. We can leave out the snakes and frogs! Grapes are good for us by themselves.

Your Turn!

⏸ Need a Review? See the *Envision It!* Skills and Strategies for additional help.

▷ Ready to Try It? As you read other text, use what you've learned about drawing conclusions and important ideas to help you understand it.

Skill

Strategy

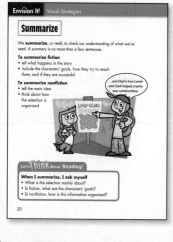

Comprehension Skill

Draw Conclusions

- You draw conclusions when you use facts and details to make decisions about characters or events.

- Think about what you already know to help you draw conclusions.

- Use what you learned about drawing conclusions and a graphic organizer like the one below as you read "What Does a Baker Do?" Then use your conclusion as the topic sentence for a paragraph that tells what a baker does.

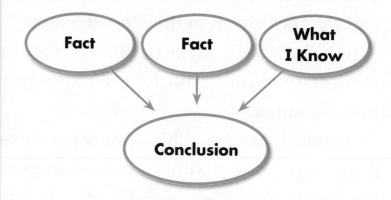

Comprehension Strategy

Summarize

Active readers summarize to help them understand. To summarize, tell the most important ideas or events in logical order, maintaining the meaning of what you read.

What Does a Baker Do?

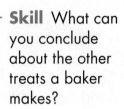

Have you ever helped an adult bake something? A baker is a person who makes baked goods for a living. A baker makes bread, cakes, pies, and many other treats!

Skill What can you conclude about the other treats a baker makes?

Some bakers work in large stores, some work in small neighborhood bakeries, and some work in restaurants. Baked goods must be fresh, so bakers often get up early in the morning to make goods to be sold that day.

Bakers need to know what kinds of treats people in their neighborhood like. This helps them know what to make and how much.

Skill How do bakers find out what customers want?

Many bakers learn their job by working with experienced bakers. They watch, listen, and practice on the job. Some bakers go to special schools to learn how to bake.

Some bakers like to experiment and create their own recipes for their customers' favorite baked goods. Working as a baker can be an exciting career!

Strategy Summarize the selection. Include why the author concludes that being a baker is an exciting career.

Your Turn!

Need a Review? See the *Envision It!* Skills and Strategies for additional help.

Ready to Try It? As you read other text, use what you've learned about drawing conclusions and summarizing to help you understand it.

Fact and Opinion

A statement of fact can be proven true or false.
A statement of opinion tells someone's ideas or feelings.

Many ants collect seeds to feed other ants in their nest.

Fact

Opinion

Wow, this is awesome!

60

How to Identify Fact and Opinion

A statement of fact can be proven true or false. An opinion tells someone's ideas or feelings. Opinions often have clue words, such as *best* or *should*.

See It!

- Look at the picture on page 60. What fact is being expressed? What opinion is being expressed?

- Look for clue words that hint that a statement is an opinion. Notice words such as *great* or *boring* that describe someone's beliefs or feelings.

Say It!

- Tell a partner one fact and one opinion about something you know about. Have your partner identify which statement is a fact and which statement is an opinion.

- Tell a partner a statement of fact. Then have your partner change your statement of fact to a statement of opinion instead. Then switch roles with your partner.

Do It!

- Use a graphic organizer like the one below to help you organize facts and opinions in a text.

Facts	Opinions

- Write a paragraph that tells about what you did in the morning before school. Include facts and opinions.

Objectives

● Examine and make judgments from the facts in the article, and support your conclusions with evidence.
● Use your prior knowledge and details from a text to make inferences about the text and support your inferences with evidence from the text.

Envision It! Skill Strategy

Skill

Strategy

Comprehension Skill

Fact and Opinion

- A fact can be proved true or false.

- An opinion gives someone's thoughts or feelings about something. An opinion cannot be proved true or false.

- Use what you learned about fact and opinion and the chart below as you read "Looking at Rocks." Then choose one fact from your chart. Use a reference source to prove the fact true or false.

Facts	Opinions

Comprehension Strategy

Inferring

When you infer, you combine your background knowledge with ideas in the text to come up with your own idea about what the author is trying to present. Active readers infer the ideas, morals, lessons, and themes of a written work.

LOOKING AT ROCKS

Looking at rocks is fun and interesting. Some rocks look the same all over. They are made of one thing. However, most rocks do not look the same all over. Some have different colors. Some have sparkles. Others have shiny spots. The colors and sparkles and shine come from the different materials mixed together in the rock.

Skill What opinion is expressed in this paragraph? What words tell you that it is an opinion?

If you like looking at rocks, you can get a job working with rocks when you grow up. Some scientists look at rocks to find out about people from long ago. Other scientists look at rocks to find oil. Some rock scientists help builders make buildings safe. Others try to predict when an earthquake will happen or a volcano will erupt.

Strategy How do you think rock scientists can help builders make safe buildings?

Rocks can tell us many things. Take a look!

Your Turn!

⏸ **Need a Review?** See the *Envision It!* Skills and Strategies for additional help.

▶ **Ready to Try It?** As you read other text, use what you've learned about fact and opinion and inferring to help you understand it.

Objectives

• Ask questions, clear up anything you don't understand, and look for facts and details. Support your answers with details from the text.

Envision It! | Skill Strategy

Skill

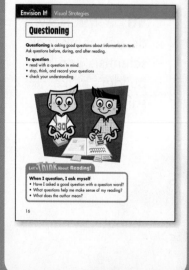

Strategy

Comprehension Skill

🎯 Fact and Opinion

- A statement of fact can be proved true or false.

- A statement of opinion cannot be proved true or false. It is a belief or judgment.

- Use what you learned about fact and opinion and a chart like the one below as you read "Swim!" Then write a short paragraph about swimmers.

Statement	Fact? How Can It Be Checked?	Opinion? What Are Clue Words?

Comprehension Strategy

🎯 Questioning

As you read, ask questions. Questioning helps you identify what you don't understand. Continue to read to find an answer to your question. You can ask literal questions about details in a selection. You can ask interpretive and evaluative questions that you have to think about and answer on your own.

Swim!

Exercise is important for good health. When people do not exercise, their muscles become soft and weak.

Swimming is one of the best ways to exercise. When swimming, you must move against the water. This makes muscles stronger. It takes more energy to move through water than it does through air. So swimming helps people lose fat. All this also helps your heart get and stay strong.

Many people get hurt playing soccer, football, or basketball. Not in swimming! It's one of the safest ways to exercise.

Swimming is also a great way to have fun while you exercise. You can cool off on a hot summer day and play water games with your friends. Swimming races are an exciting way to beat the heat.

If you do not know how to swim, you should learn how—now!

Skill What reference could you use to see whether these statements are true?

Strategy What questions can you ask about swimming as a way to have fun? How can you answer your questions?

Your Turn!

⏸ **Need a Review?** See the *Envision It!* Skills and Strategies for additional help.

▶ **Ready to Try It?** As you read other text, use what you've learned about fact and opinion and questioning to help you understand it.

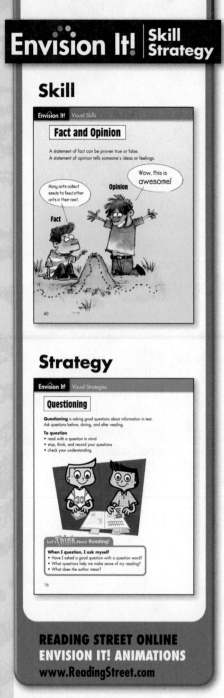

Comprehension Skill

🎯 Fact and Opinion

• A statement of fact tells something that can be proven true or false. You can prove it by reading a reference source.

• A statement of opinion tells someone's ideas or feelings. Words that tell feelings, such as *should* or *best*, are clue words.

• Use what you learned about fact and opinion and a chart like the one below as you read "Coming to America." Then use the facts to draw a conclusion about immigrants in America.

Fact	How to Prove

Opinion	Clue Words

Comprehension Strategy

🎯 Questioning

Active readers use questions to help them understand what they read. While you read, ask literal questions to make sure you understand. You can also ask yourself questions using what you already know or have read to interpret, connect to, or evaluate what you are reading.

Coming to America

The country where you were born is called your *homeland*. People who leave their homeland and come to another country—such as America—are called *immigrants*. America has been called a "nation of immigrants." Why?

Everyone who lives in America now (except for Native Americans) once came from somewhere else. This may have happened a very long time ago in your family. Or maybe you and your family arrived here recently.

Immigrants left their homeland for different reasons. Some came to America looking for religious freedom. Others came to escape war or hunger. But mostly, people came looking for a better life.

People came to America from all over the world, but together we are one nation!

Skill What are the facts in the paragraph? How could you prove whether they are true or false?

Strategy Ask questions to make sure you understand the text, such as *What are the different reasons people immigrate?*

Your Turn!

❚❚ **Need a Review?** See the *Envision It!* Skills and Strategies for additional help.

▶ **Ready to Try It?** As you read other text, use what you've learned about fact and opinion and questioning to help you understand it.

Generalize

How to Generalize

A generalization is a broad statement about something that is true for many examples. To generalize, look at a number of examples of something and use your prior knowledge to decide what all of the examples have in common.

See It!

- Look at the picture on the previous page. What does it tell you about making generalizations? What other generalizations can you make about birds? Use clue words, such as *many, all,* or *few.*

- Look around for objects about which you can make a generalization. For example, are there posters on the wall? What do they have in common? Make a generalization about the objects.

Say It!

- Find a statement that seems to be a generalization, and read it aloud to a partner. Together, talk about why it is a generalization.

- What kinds of generalizations have you heard before about something? Discuss with a partner or small group.

Do It!

- Use a graphic organizer such as this one to help you make generalizations as you read:

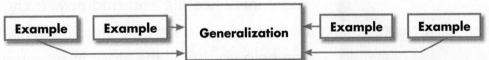

- Walk around the classroom to find related items, and write generalizations that tell what the items have in common.

Objectives

● Describe how characters relate to each other and the changes that happen to them. ● Tell in order the main events of a story. Explain how they will affect future events in a story.

Envision It! | Skill Strategy

Skill

Strategy

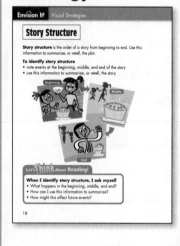

Comprehension Skill

⟳ Generalize

- When you read about how several things are alike in some way, you can make a general statement about them.

- Clue words such as *most, many, all,* or *few* signal generalizations.

- Use what you learned about generalizing and the graphic organizer below as you read "Songbirds of the Sea." What generalization can you make from the story?

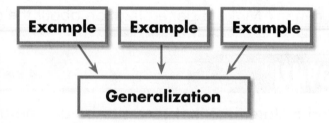

Comprehension Strategy

⟳ Story Structure

As you read, think about the events that happen at the beginning, middle, and end of the story, including how earlier events might influence the end and how a character might change. Using the structure of a story can help you retell the story in your own words and improve your comprehension.

Songbirds of the Sea

Dad always wanted to see beluga whales in the wild. I wasn't very excited about going to Canada for our vacation. "Sam, I think you might enjoy learning about the songbirds of the sea," Dad said.

"Songbirds? I thought whales lived in the water," I said.

"Many people call beluga whales songbirds because they are always making beautiful sounds," Dad said. "That's how they communicate and find food."

So, we traveled by boat on the Churchill River in late July. This river has the most beluga whales in the world.

After an hour on the boat, we spotted a pod of twenty belugas. It was incredible! They were huge. Everyone was really excited. This was more fun than I thought it would be. In fact, I would say it was the most fun I ever had on vacation! I guess learning can be fun.

Skill What clue words in this sentence signal a generalization?

Skill What generalization does the author make in this paragraph?

Strategy How do Sam's feelings change from the beginning to the end of the story?

Your Turn!

⏸ **Need a Review?** See the *Envision It!* Skills and Strategies for additional help.

▶ **Ready to Try It?** As you read other text, use what you've learned about generalizing and story structure to help you understand it.

71

Objectives
- Tell in order the main events of a story. Explain how they will affect future events in a story. • Summarize information in a text.

Skill

Strategy

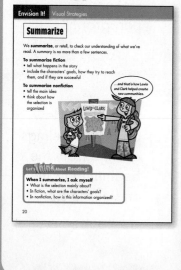

Comprehension Skill

🎯 Generalize

- When you read, you can sometimes make a general statement about what you have read.

- A general statement tells how some things are mostly alike or all alike.

- Use what you learned about generalizing as you read "Batting the Ball." Use the text and a graphic organizer like the one below to make a generalization.

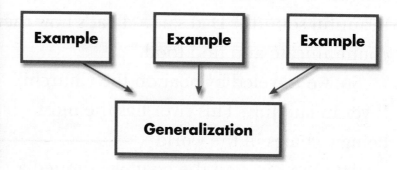

Comprehension Strategy

🎯 Summarize

Active readers sum up what happens as they read a story. When you sum up, remember to tell only the important events in the order that they happened, maintaining the meaning of the story and what the characters learned. This will help you remember what you are reading.

Batting the Ball

Betsy went to a new school at the beginning of third grade. At recess, Betsy wanted to play baseball. The teacher told Betsy that she could not play with a hard baseball, because someone might get hurt. The playground rule was that only soft balls were allowed.

Skill Can you make a generalization about school playgrounds using the details from the first paragraph?

Betsy laughed. "But I am a baseball player," she said. Betsy did not understand why she could only play with a soft ball.

A few days later, another third-grader brought a hard baseball to school. Betsy was eager to show off her baseball skills. She loved the feel of the bat as it hit the hard ball.

When it was Betsy's turn to bat, she stepped up to home plate. The pitcher threw the ball, and it curved around. The ball hit Betsy in the shoulder and she fell to the ground.

"Ouch!" Betsy cried. The teacher ran over to see what had happened. Betsy stood up, rubbing her shoulder. "I think we should use a soft ball," she said to the teacher.

"What good thinking!" the teacher said, replacing the baseball with a soft ball.

Strategy Summarize the story. What is the order of events? What are the results of Betsy's actions?

Your Turn!

Need a Review? See the *Envision It!* Skills and Strategies for additional help.

Ready to Try It? As you read other text, use what you've learned about generalizing and summarizing to help you understand it.

Objectives

- Examine and make judgments from the facts in the article, and support your conclusions with evidence.
- Use your prior knowledge and details from a text to make inferences about the text and support your inferences with evidence from the text.

Envision It! | Skill Strategy

Skill

Strategy

Comprehension Skill

◉ Generalize

- A general statement, or generalization, tells how some things are mostly or all alike.

- Key words, such as *always*, *never*, and *most*, signal a generalization.

- Be sure you can support your generalization with facts and logic.

- Use what you learned about generalizing and a graphic organizer like the one below as you read "The Famous Thinker, Plato." Then write a short paragraph explaining your generalization and support it with details from the text.

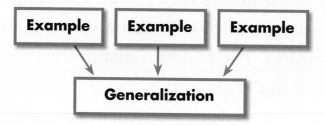

Comprehension Strategy

◉ Inferring

Active readers use what they know and the ideas and clues in what they read to come up with their own ideas about what the author presents. Making inferences can help you understand the text better.

THE FAMOUS THINKER, PLATO

One of the most famous thinkers of the ancient world was Plato. He was a Greek man who lived about 2,400 years ago. Plato was a student of another famous thinker, Socrates. Some ideas about our world today started with Plato and Socrates.

How did Plato learn so much? Besides studying many writings, Plato traveled far. He observed much on his journeys. Then Plato began a school of science and philosophy. Philosophy is the study of how our minds gather knowledge. This school became a model for today's colleges.

Many of Plato's writings have survived through history. He wrote mostly letters and dialogues. His writing covered many topics, including politics, nature, and happiness. In school, you will likely read some of Plato's famous writings. They have been part of many students' educations for hundreds of years.

Strategy Why do you think that the teachings of Plato are still popular today?

Skill What generalization can you make about the writings of Plato? Use a key word, such as *always*, in your answer.

Your Turn!

❚❚ Need a Review? See the *Envision It!* Skills and Strategies for additional help.

▶ Ready to Try It? As you read other text, use what you've learned about generalizing and inferring to help you understand it.

Main Idea and Details

What is the selection all about? What details support the main idea?

How to Identify Main Idea and Details

The main idea is what a piece of writing is mostly about.
Details explain the main idea or give more information about it.

See It!

- Look at page 76. Imagine that the main idea of the picture is how people use telescopes to see objects in space. What details are pictured that give more information about this main idea?
- Use illustrations, graphs, and other images to help you figure out the main idea. How do they help you tell the main idea?

Say It!

- With a partner, state the main idea of a piece of writing. Then come up with at least one example from the reading that supports, proves, or explains this statement.
- To check if you have correctly identified the main idea, tell it to a partner after reading. Ask: "Does this make sense? Does it cover all the important details?"

Do It!

- Use a web like the one below to identify the main idea and details.

- Write about your favorite hobby. After writing, circle the main idea and underline details that tell more about it.

Envision It! | Skill Strategy

Skill

Strategy

Comprehension Skill

Main Idea and Details

- The topic is what a piece of writing is about. The main idea is the most important idea about the topic.

- Supporting details are small pieces of information that tell more about the main idea.

- Use what you know about main idea and details and the graphic organizer below as you read "The Coldest Continent." Then use the graphic organizer to help you write a one-paragraph summary.

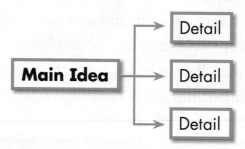

Comprehension Strategy

Monitor and Clarify

While you are reading, it's important for you to know when you understand something and when you don't. If you are confused, stop and reread the section aloud. Looking back and reading is one way to clarify or adjust your understanding.

78

The Coldest Continent

Antarctica is not like any other continent. It is as far south as you can go on Earth. The South Pole is found there. Ice covers the whole land. In some places the ice is almost three miles thick! Beneath the ice are mountains and valleys.

The weather in Antarctica is harsh. It is the coldest place on Earth. The temperature does not get above freezing. It is also one of the windiest places in the world.

Not many living things are found in Antarctica. People go there to study for only a short time. Very few animals can live there. Yet many animals live on nearby islands. Seals and penguins swim in the ocean waters. They build nests on the land. Some birds spend their summers in Antarctica. But most of the continent is just ice, snow, and cold air.

Skill Read the title and the first sentence. What do you think is the main idea?

Strategy Why can very few animals live in Antarctica? If you don't understand, how can you clarify or adjust your comprehension?

Your Turn!

⏸ **Need a Review?** See the *Envision It!* Skills and Strategies for additional help.

▶ **Ready to Try It?** As you read other text, use what you've learned about main idea and details and monitoring and clarifying to help you understand it.

Skill

Strategy

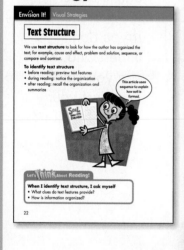

Comprehension Skill

Main Idea and Details

• The topic is what a piece of writing is all about. The main idea is the most important idea about the topic.

• Details and facts are small pieces of information. They tell more about the main idea.

• Use what you learned about main idea and details and the graphic organizer below as you read "Do All Birds Fly?" Then write a short paragraph explaining whether all birds fly.

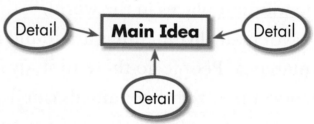

Comprehension Strategy

Text Structure

Good readers look for how a text is structured, or organized, to help them understand the information. A compare-and-contrast structure explains how things are alike and different. Other structures authors use include description, cause-and-effect, and question-and-answer formats.

Do All Birds Fly?

Birds are Alike

There are many different kinds of birds in the world. But all birds are alike in some ways. All birds lay eggs. All birds have feathers. And all birds have wings.

Penguins and Ostriches

Just because all birds have wings does not mean that all birds can fly. Penguins are birds but they do not fly. They use their wings to swim. Penguins are not the only birds that do not fly. Some large birds, like the ostrich, do not fly. They move about only by walking.

Strategy How do the headings better help you understand how the text is structured?

The Frigate

Some birds fly but hardly ever walk. The frigate is a bird that does not walk very well. It also does not swim. It gets from place to place only by flying.

Ducks

Most birds, however, combine flying with some kind of walking or swimming. Ducks can do three things. They can fly, walk, and swim. Perhaps that is why we sometimes say, "What a lucky duck!"

Skill What facts and details does this paragraph include about the frigate?

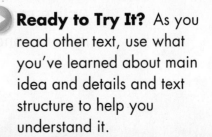

Your Turn!

⏸ **Need a Review?** See the *Envision It! Skills and Strategies* for additional help.

▶ **Ready to Try It?** As you read other text, use what you've learned about main idea and details and text structure to help you understand it.

Objectives
- Identify the topic and find the author's purposes for writing.
- Identify the details or facts that support the main idea. • Use your prior knowledge and details from a text to make inferences and support them with evidence from the text.

Skill

Strategy

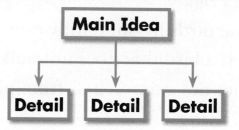

Comprehension Skill

Main Idea and Details

- The topic is what a piece of writing is about. The main idea is the most important idea about the topic.

- Details are pieces of information that tell more about the main idea.

- Use what you learned about main idea and details and a graphic organizer like the one below as you read "The Best Game." Then use the graphic organizer to help you write a summary of the text.

Main Idea

Detail **Detail** **Detail**

Comprehension Strategy

Inferring

When you infer, you combine your background knowledge with evidence in the text to come up with your own ideas or conclusions about what the author is saying. Active readers infer the ideas, morals, lessons, and themes of a written work.

The Best Game

I think board games are the best family activity. Playing a board game with family or friends is my favorite thing to do on a rainy day. However, my sister doesn't agree. She likes playing charades with a group. To her, board games are boring.

Board games include everything you need right in the box. There is nothing to think up or to make. The rules are printed out. That's the best part! There shouldn't be any arguments among players. Thousands of board games are sold every year. The people who buy them can't all be wrong.

On the other hand, my sister says charades is a creative game. Players must think of books, movies, or songs that will stump the other team. Players have a great time using their imagination and acting.

Here you have two kinds of games, two people, and two ideas. Which game is best? You decide.

Strategy What do you think the author is trying to persuade you to think or do?

Skill What details does this paragraph include about board games?

Strategy Who do you think is better at charades—the narrator or the sister? Why do you think so?

Your Turn!

⏸ **Need a Review?** See the *Envision It!* Skills and Strategies for additional help.

▶ **Ready to Try It?** As you read other text, use what you've learned about main idea and details and inferring to help you understand it.

83

Graphic Sources

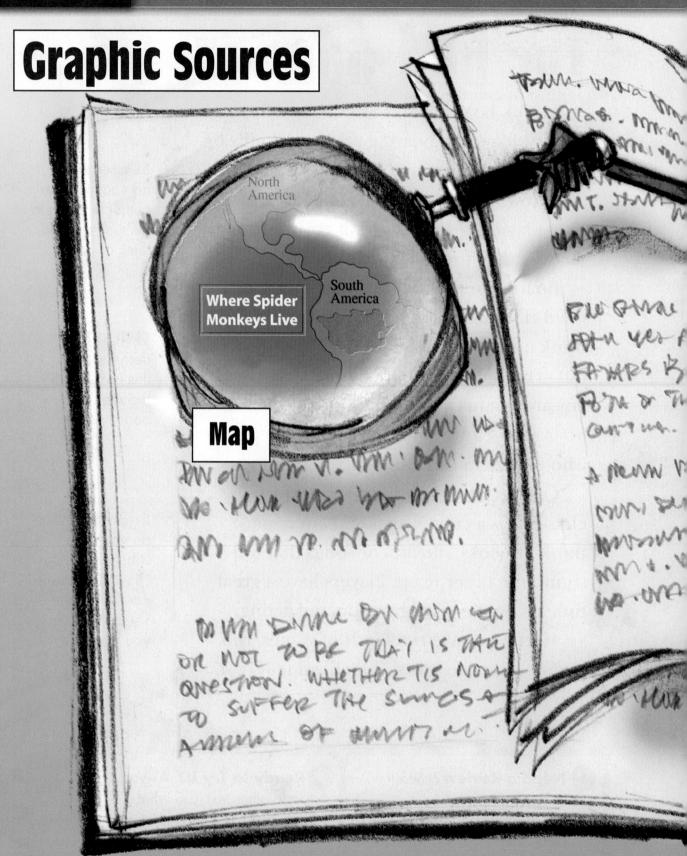

North America

Where Spider Monkeys Live

South America

Map

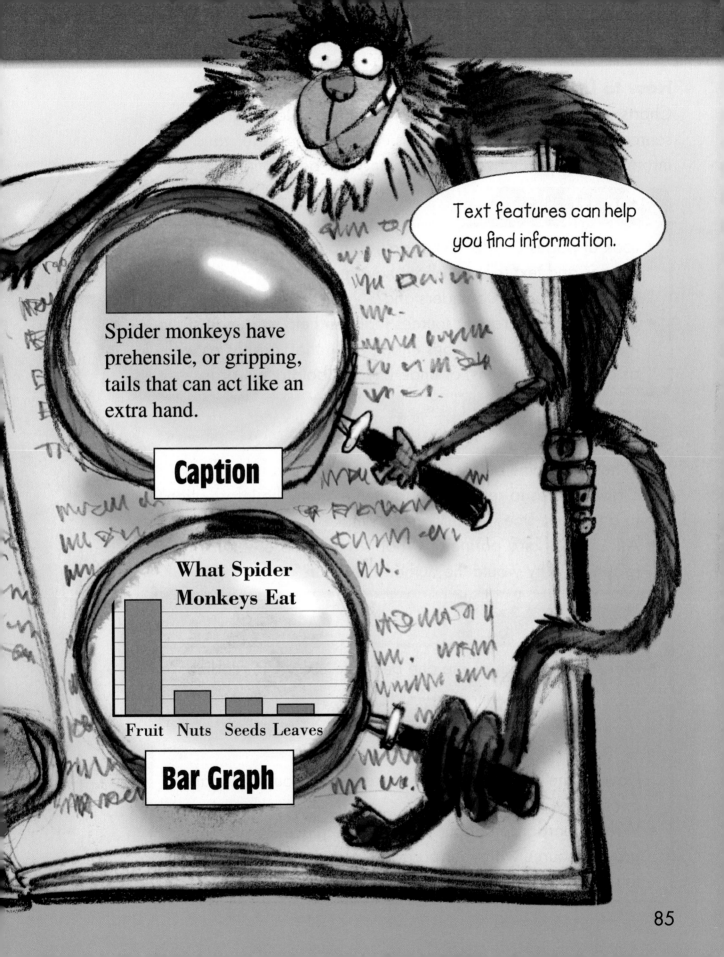

85

How to Use Graphic Sources

Charts, diagrams, maps, and graphs are examples of graphic sources, or features. These features can help you understand information or predict what the reading will be about.

See It!

- Look at pages 84–85. What do you notice? What do the images and text tell you about how graphic sources make information easier to understand?
- Scan a text for graphic sources that can help you understand the topic. Look for captions underneath photographs as well as charts, illustrations, or underlined or boldface words.

Say It!

- When you come across a graphic source as you read, take a few minutes to review it, and then explain the information to a partner. Does the information make sense?
- Ask yourself or a partner, "What is the purpose of this graphic? Why would the author include it?"

Do It!

- Make a chart such as the one below to use while reading:

Type of Graphic Source	What It Shows	How It Helps You Understand Information

  How do the different graphic sources help you understand information?
- Write a paragraph about your favorite place. Include a graphic source with your paragraph, such as a map of how to get there.

Spider monkeys have prehensile, or gripping, tails that can act like an extra hand.

What Spider Monkeys Eat

Fruit   Nuts   Seeds   Leaves

Skill

Strategy

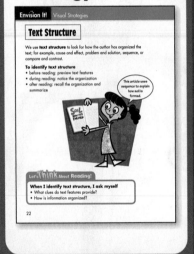

Comprehension Skill

🎯 Graphic Sources

- Graphic sources help you understand information that is in the text and give extra information.

- Maps, charts, illustrations, and captions make information easier to understand.

- Use what you learned about graphic sources and the chart below as you read "Patterns in the Sky." Then write a paragraph telling what you learned about constellations and how they were named.

Type of Graphic Source	What It Shows	How It Helps You Understand Information

Comprehension Strategy

🎯 Text Structure

Good readers look at the way information is organized, or structured, to help them understand what they read. Some selections are descriptions. Headings can help you know what is being described. Other structures are cause-and-effect, compare-and-contrast, and question-and-answer.

Patterns in the Sky

Constellations

Long ago, people looked up at the night sky and noticed patterns in the stars. They gave these patterns names, such as *Libra* and *Pisces*. Today we call these patterns *constellations*.

The Big Dipper

The Big Dipper is a star pattern that has inspired many stories. The seven stars of the Big Dipper are part of a constellation called *Ursa Major*. It is one of the most recognizable patterns in the sky. People have told stories about this group of stars for hundreds of years.

Other Names

Many of the names of the constellations come from old stories. *Hercules* is named after a brave hero from a Greek story. *Leo* is named for a lion with skin so strong that no weapon could harm it.

Where to Find Them

One reason that constellations were given names was for people to remember them. This helped people long ago understand how the movement of the Earth was connected to seasons.

Libra

Skill What does the diagram show you that isn't in the text? Why is the caption needed?

Strategy Headings can help you figure out how the text is organized. What does this paragraph describe?

Your Turn!

⏸ **Need a Review?** See the *Envision It!* Skills and Strategies for additional help.

▶ **Ready to Try It?** As you read other text, use what you've learned about graphic sources and text structure to help you understand it.

Envision It! | Skill Strategy

Skill

Strategy

Comprehension Skill

Graphic Sources

- Graphic sources are ways of showing information visually, or in a way you can see.

- Charts, diagrams, maps, and graphs are examples of graphic sources, or features.

- Graphic sources can help you predict what the reading will be about.

- Use what you learned about graphic sources to read "Largest U.S. Cities." Then use the text and the bar graph to make a new graph showing how the population of New York City compares to Los Angeles, Chicago, and Houston combined.

Comprehension Strategy

Important Ideas

Before you read a selection or story, look for the important ideas in titles, topic sentences, key words, charts, or photos and other illustrations. While you read, stop and ask, "What is this text all about?" Important ideas summarize a selection or tell what it is all about. Try to find the most important idea in each paragraph and verify your predictions.

Largest U.S. Cities

New York

Los Angeles

Chicago

Houston

Millions of people in the United States live in cities. The number of people who live in a city is called its population.

The U.S. city with the most people living in it is New York City. Los Angeles, California, comes in second. Chicago, Illinois, is the third largest city with Houston, Texas, closely following. New York City, however, has almost as many people as Los Angeles, Chicago, and Houston put together!

Strategy What are two important ideas in the text?

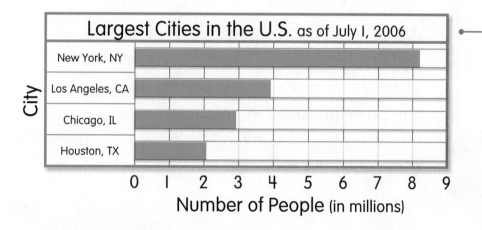

Largest Cities in the U.S. as of July 1, 2006

City
- New York, NY
- Los Angeles, CA
- Chicago, IL
- Houston, TX

Number of People (in millions)
0 1 2 3 4 5 6 7 8 9

Skill Look at the bar graph. What facts can you learn from the graph?

Your Turn!

⏸ **Need a Review?** See the *Envision It!* Skills and Strategies for additional help.

▶ **Ready to Try It?** As you read other text, use what you've learned about graphic sources and important ideas to help you understand it.

Objectives

● Look for and use information found in graphics. ● Find and use information by following and explaining a set of written directions with many steps.

Envision It! | Skill Strategy

Skill

Strategy

Comprehension Skill

Graphic Sources

- Graphic sources are ways of showing information visually, or in a way you can see. They provide additional information to the text.

- Charts, photos, diagrams, and maps are all graphic sources.

- Use what you learned about graphic sources as you read "Ancient Cave Murals." Then, using the procedural text and the color wheel, write a paragraph explaining the steps to make purple paint.

Comprehension Strategy

Important Ideas

Active readers look for graphic sources and text features that often present important ideas. An author's most important ideas can be emphasized in graphic sources. Graphic sources help readers better understand the text.

Ancient Cave Murals

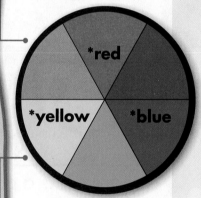

In 1940, four teenage boys discovered a cave covered with murals of animals. People had painted the murals about 17,000 years ago. Scientists studied the cave paintings and found that the ancient artists made their paint using pigment, which is a powder that gives paint its color. They were able to make very few colors of paint.

There are only three primary colors that, along with black and white, make all other colors. Today we can buy or make any color of paint we want!

Skill What colors do you see in the murals?

Strategy What important idea is shown by the color wheel?

*red

*yellow   *blue

*primary color

How to Make Green Paint

1. Choose yellow and blue paint pigment.
2. Add water or oil and mix it together.
3. Add black or white pigment to make the green darker or lighter.
4. Add more blue or more yellow until you have a green you like!

Skill What colors would you add together to make orange? Try it in art class!

Your Turn!

❚❚ **Need a Review?** See the *Envision It!* Skills and Strategies for additional help.

▶ **Ready to Try It?** As you read other text, use what you've learned about graphic sources and important ideas to help you understand it.

93

Literary Elements

Characters

A character is a person or animal in a story.

Setting

The setting is the time and place in which a story happens.

Plot

A story's plot is the important events that happen.
The plot starts with a problem and ends with a solution.

Theme

The theme is the big idea of a story.

How to Identify Literary Elements

Stories are made up of the following parts: characters, setting, theme, and plot.

See It!

- Look for hints about a story's characters, setting, theme, or plot in the illustrations or other graphic elements of a text. How are the characters shown in the illustrations? What do the illustrations tell you about the setting? Do the images fit with the descriptions?
- Visualize as you read an author's descriptions of characters and setting. Try to picture in your mind what the author is describing.

Say It!

- With a partner, read aloud the text on pages 94–95. What do you learn about characters, setting, theme, and plot?
- Think about a story you have read or movie you have seen recently. Tell a partner what the characters, setting, theme, and plot of the story are. If you are having trouble describing the theme, think about what the big idea of the story was, and tell it in your own words.
- Divide into groups of four. Each group member should choose a different literary element on which to focus as he or she reads an agreed-upon short story. Then each member should discuss the literary element he or she chose in relation to the story.

Do It!

- After reading, make a list of the important events that happen first, next, and last in a story. What problems do the characters face? How are those problems resolved? Use a graphic organizer like the one below to identify the events in a story, or plot:

| Problem | → | Solution |

- What do you imagine the characters and setting of a story look like? Draw a picture of the characters or setting and include a caption underneath that gives a brief description.

Envision It! Skill Strategy

Skill

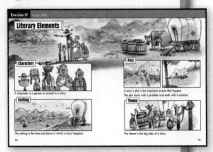

Strategy

READING STREET ONLINE
ENVISION IT! ANIMATIONS
www.ReadingStreet.com

Comprehension Skill

Literary Elements: Character, Setting, and Theme

- A character is a person or animal in a story. You learn about characters, how they change, and their relationships from their actions and what they say.

- The setting is when and where a story takes place.

- The theme is what you learn from the story and can be supported with details.

- Use what you learned about character, setting, and theme as you read "Flash to Bang." Fill out a chart like the one below using details from the story.

Story Title	
Characters	**Setting**

Comprehension Strategy

Background Knowledge

Good readers connect what they are reading with what they already know. Using what you know can help you monitor and adjust your comprehension as you read.

Flash to Bang

Thomas stood in the yard and looked up at a big dark cloud. He could see lightning in the distance. It would probably rain soon. All week the weather had been sunny and warm. Now it was Saturday—no school, no karate practice, no piano lesson—and he really wanted to spend the day playing outside.

"Why can't I stay outside?" he asked his mom. "I don't mind getting wet."

"It's not the rain I'm worried about," she told him as they went inside. "Lightning is dangerous, and the storm is coming closer."

"How can you tell?" Thomas wondered.

"Lightning causes thunder," his mom replied, "but it takes time for the sound of the thunder to reach us. When you see lightning, count the seconds until you hear the thunder. For every five seconds you count, the lightning is about one mile away."

During the storm, they counted seconds from seeing the flash of lightning to hearing the bang of thunder. Thomas learned something new and had fun with his mom.

Skill What details does the first paragraph give about the setting? What details does it give about Thomas?

Strategy What do you know about storms? Why shouldn't you play outside in a storm?

Skill Describe the interaction between Thomas and his mom. How does she help Thomas change by the end? What details tell you the theme?

Your Turn!

Need a Review? See the *Envision It!* Skills and Strategies for additional help.

Ready to Try It? As you read other text, use what you've learned about literary elements and background knowledge to understand it.

99

Envision It! Skill Strategy

Skill

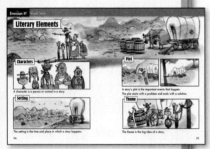

Strategy

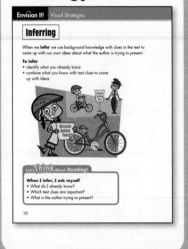

Comprehension Skill

🎯 Literary Elements: Character, Setting, and Plot

- A character is a person or animal in a story. Authors usually describe characters, and you can also learn more about them, their relationships, and how they change from their actions and what they say.

- The setting is when and where a story takes place.

- The plot of a story includes what happens at the beginning, middle, and end. Earlier events usually influence the end.

- Use what you learned about these literary elements and the chart below as you read "An Up-and-Down Story."

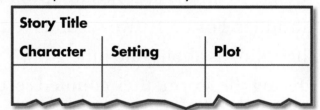

Story Title		
Character	**Setting**	**Plot**

Comprehension Strategy

🎯 Inferring

As you read, use facts and details from the author and what you already know to come up with your own ideas. Inferring helps you connect to the story.

AN UP-AND-DOWN STORY

"Timber!" I heard Dad yell. I ran to my bedroom window and saw one of the trees in our backyard come crashing to Earth. It just missed hitting the garage.

Mom and I rushed outside. "What in the world are you doing now?" Mom asked.

Dad set down his axe and said, "I'm making a story pole!" Mom rolled her eyes.

Skill Who are the characters in this story? What is the setting?

Last summer we visited a place in Olympia, Washington, that had a story pole. Chief Shelton had carved animal figures into a cedar tree. The pole tells a story about Chief Shelton's Snohomish culture. He worked on it for five years. When he died in 1938, other people in the tribe finished the carvings. "Can I help?" I asked.

Skill What is the plot of the story?

"Sure, Billy!" Dad said.

"So, what kind of animal should we put at the top of our pole?" I asked.

"How about a mule?" Mom suggested.

Strategy How can you tell how Mom feels about Dad's project?

Your Turn!

⏸ **Need a Review?** See the *Envision It!* Skills and Strategies for additional help.

▶ **Ready to Try It?** As you read other text, use what you've learned about literary elements and inferring to help you understand it.

Envision It! | Skill Strategy

Skill

Plot

A story's plot is the important events that happen. The plot starts with a problem and ends with a solution.

Theme

The theme is the big idea of a story.

95

Strategy

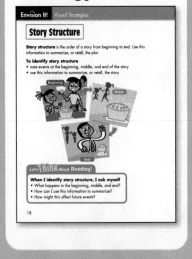

Envision It! Visual Strategies

Story Structure

Story structure is the order of a story from beginning to end. Use this information to summarize, or retell, the plot.

To identify story structure
- note events at the beginning, middle, and end of the story
- use this information to summarize, or retell, the story

Beginning

Middle

End

Let's **think** About Reading!

When I identify story structure, I ask myself
- What happens in the beginning, middle, and end?
- How can I use this information to summarize?
- How might this affect future events?

18

Comprehension Skill

🔘 Literary Elements: Plot and Theme

- The important events in the beginning, middle, and end of a story make up the plot.

- The theme is the "big idea" or lesson in the story.

- Use what you learned about plot and theme and a graphic organizer like the one below as you read "The Ant and the Beetle." Then write the theme of the story, using just one sentence.

Beginning → **Middle** → **End**

Comprehension Strategy

🔘 Story Structure

Good readers look for what happens in the beginning, middle, and end of a story. Authors usually write in time order, using sequence words to show the order of events.

The Ant and the Beetle

Adapted from Aesop's "The Fox and the Crow"

Annie Ant stole a piece of cheese from an abandoned picnic and scrambled up on a rock. She was about to eat the cheese when she noticed a beetle nearby. The beetle had a plan.

"My, my, I have never seen such a beautiful ant," flattered the beetle. "From the tip of your antennae to the end of your abdomen, you are simply gorgeous!"

"Finally, someone appreciates my beauty!" Annie thought.

"You must be delicate," continued the beetle. "Surely you are not strong enough to help the other ants."

"Hmph!" said the insulted ant. To show him, Annie set down the cheese and lifted a huge rock over her head.

The beetle grabbed the cheese and began to scurry away. "Yes, you are strong, but you are also foolish."

Strategy Note the time order clues *about to* and *when*. How did the author structure this story?

Skill Summarize the plot. What lesson did Annie learn at the end of the story?

Your Turn!

Need a Review? See the *Envision It!* Skills and Strategies for additional help.

Ready to Try It? As you read other text, use what you've learned about plot, theme, and story structure to help you understand it.

Sequence

The sequence of a selection is the order of events.

First

Next

Last

How to Identify Sequence

The sequence is the order in which things happen in a story—what happens first, next, and last.

See It!

- Look at a story that has illustrations or other images. Do they give you any clues about what happens first, next, and last? Use the pictures to help you understand sequence while you read.

- Look for clue words, such as *first, next, then,* or *after.* They will help tell you the order of a story.

Say It!

- With a partner, take turns telling what happens first, next, and last in a story.

- Ask a classmate to paraphrase, or tell in his or her own words, what happens in a story from beginning to end. How does this help you understand the order of events of the story?

Do It!

- Draw images of a story's events on a sheet of paper or a computer program. Be sure to put your illustrations in order of first, next, and last to identify sequence.

- Make a sequence diagram or a time line to help you keep track of the most important events in the story.

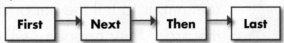

- In groups, perform skits. Each group should take a different part of a story to act out.

Skill

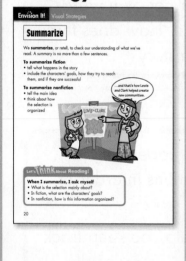

Strategy

Comprehension Skill

◎ Sequence

- Sequence is the order in which the main events in the plot happen—what occurs first, next, and last.

- Sometimes a writer uses clue words such as *first, next,* and *in the morning* or *at night.* Sometimes a writer does not. Then you can tell the order by picturing in your mind what is happening.

- Use what you learned about sequence and the graphic organizer below as you read "Chores." Use the text and the graphic organizer to help you summarize the story events as you read.

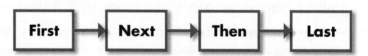

First → **Next** → **Then** → **Last**

Comprehension Strategy

◎ Summarize

Good readers summarize what happens as they read a story. When you sum up, remember to tell the important events in the order they happen, without losing the meaning of the text. This will help you remember what you're reading.

Chores

Louisa looked at the chores list. It was her turn to fold the laundry. That was the chore she disliked most. How could she get out of it?

Louisa saw her brother J. B. in his room. "J. B., would you like to make some money?" Louisa asked.

"What's the catch?" asked J. B.

"I'll pay you 50 cents to fold the …," Louisa stopped. She remembered that she had spent her 50 cents yesterday. "Never mind."

Next Louisa saw her sister Grace pouting in the living room.

"I got the worst chore on the list today," said Grace. "I don't like dusting furniture!"

"Dusting furniture isn't bad. I have to fold the laundry! *That's* the worst!" Louisa said.

"I don't mind folding laundry," said Grace. "Anything but dusting!"

The two girls looked at each other. They both smiled. As Grace folded the laundry, Louisa hummed and dusted.

Strategy Here's a good place to stop and summarize the sequence of the plot's events so far.

Skill This paragraph begins with a time-order transition word. What happens after Louisa talks to J. B.?

Your Turn!

⏸ **Need a Review?** See the *Envision It!* Skills and Strategies for additional help.

▶ **Ready to Try It?** As you read other text, use what you've learned about sequence and summarizing to help you understand it.

Envision It! | Skill Strategy

Skill

Strategy

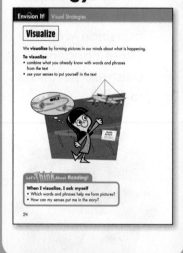

Comprehension Skill

🎯 Sequence

- Sequence is the order in which events happen in a story.

- As you read, look for clue words that tell time, or words such as *first, then, next, after that,* and *finally,* to understand the sequence of events.

- A time line can help you keep track of the sequence of events.

- Use what you learned about sequence and the graphic organizer below as you read "Nalukataq, the Blanket Toss."

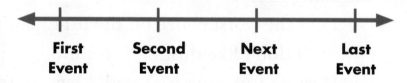

| First Event | Second Event | Next Event | Last Event |

Comprehension Strategy

🎯 Visualize

While you are reading, you can use the text to form pictures in your mind. This helps you understand and keep track of the details of what you read. Use language that appeals to your senses and other descriptions to help you create the images. If you have trouble visualizing what you are reading, reread the text until you can picture it in your mind.

NALUKATAQ, THE BLANKET TOSS

It is the end of June in Wainwright, Alaska. The whole village has come together for *Nalukataq*. This is the celebration of a good whale-hunting season. The people are glad that the whaling crew has returned.

The event begins with visiting and a big feast. Then there are games, followed by music and dancing that go late into the night. One of the games is the blanket toss. In fact, the celebration is named for this event.

The nalukataq is a large round blanket made from walrus or seal skins. It has heavy rope handles. First, about 15 people come together around the blanket. They lift it up. Then a person stands in the middle. The people holding the blanket toss and catch the person. The first jumper is always the captain of the crew that killed the whale.

The tradition comes from long ago. The blanket toss was once used in hunting. While a hunter was high in the air, he could see into the distance to find whales.

Skill What is the first thing that happens at the celebration? Add this to your time line.

Strategy What do you see in your mind as you think about the blanket toss? What should you do if you can't picture it?

Skill What clue words in this paragraph show the sequence of the blanket toss?

Your Turn!

⏸ **Need a Review?** See the *Envision It!* Skills and Strategies for additional help.

▶ **Ready to Try It?** As you read other text, use what you've learned about sequence and visualizing to help you understand it.

Objectives
- Tell in order the main events of a story. Explain how they will affect future events in a story.
- Monitor your comprehension of a text and adjust your reading based on how well you understand what you are reading.

Envision It! | Skill Strategy

Skill

Strategy

Comprehension Skill

Sequence

- To sequence the events in a story, tell the order in which events happen.

- Transition words such as *first, next, then,* and *finally* are often used to sequence events in a story.

- Use what you learned about sequence and a graphic organizer like the one below as you read "Moving Day." Then write a paragraph to summarize the story in order, maintaining the meaning of the story.

Comprehension Strategy

Monitor and Clarify

When reading, stop after a paragraph or two and ask, "What did I learn?" "What doesn't make sense?" and "How does this connect to what I already know?" Reread aloud to clarify or read on to look for answers. Monitoring and clarifying will help you understand what you read.

MOVING DAY

Tom's family was getting ready to move to Chicago. Tom's mom was starting a new job in two weeks. There was a lot to do to get ready for moving day!

Mom and Dad decided to pack things that they didn't need every day. Tom would help. First, he helped his dad pack tools in the garage. After that, Tom helped his mom carefully wrap special treasures from the attic. When they were done, the house seemed strange and there were boxes everywhere.

The day before moving day Tom got up early to pack his own clothes. After lunch, Tom packed all of his toys and other belongings. When Tom went to bed that night, his room was almost empty.

Moving day finally arrived. While the movers loaded all of their belongings into the truck, Tom helped his parents make sure nothing was forgotten. It had been a tremendous amount of work to get ready for moving day!

Skill Here are some clue words. In what sequence have events happened so far?

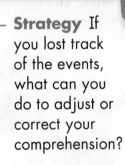

Strategy If you lost track of the events, what can you do to adjust or correct your comprehension?

Your Turn!

❚❚ Need a Review? See the *Envision It!* Skills and Strategies for additional help.

▷ Ready to Try It? As you read other text, use what you've learned about sequence and monitoring and clarifying to help you understand it.

Classify and Categorize

Classifying or categorizing means putting things that are related into groups.

Forest Life | Desert Life

112

How to Classify and Categorize

When we classify and categorize, we put things into groups based on how they are alike.

See It!

- Picture people, places, or things from your reading. Sketch what you see in your mind on a piece of paper. After drawing these items, sort them into groups.

- Look at items around the classroom. What things are related to each other? With a partner, make a list of the things you see that you can put into groups.

Say It!

- Picture a place you have been before, such as a park, grocery store, or school. With a partner, name things that you see there. For example, you might see apples, bananas, milk, and juice at a grocery store. Take turns naming items and placing them into groups.

Do It!

- Make a graphic organizer like the one below. Use it to help you classify and categorize information on a topic.

Fruit	Vegetables
bananas, apples, limes, raspberries	broccoli, green beans, lettuce

- With your teacher, gather small items around the classroom that you can easily classify and categorize. Sort the objects by shape, by color, by how you use them, and so on.

Steps in a Process

Steps in a Process

Steps in a process tell how to make, do, or explain something in order from first to last.

See It!

- Look at the picture on page 114. Can you follow the steps pictured? Tell what happens first, next, and last.
- To follow the steps in a process, look for signal words, such as *first, next, then, last, begin,* and *end,* that show the order of the steps.
- Look in cookbooks or on signs for text that uses pictures to show the steps in a process. Why might pictures be helpful?

Say It!

- Think of a simple game you like to play. Take turns with a partner giving step-by-step directions on how to play the game.
- With a partner, discuss why clear directions are important.

Do It!

- On strips of paper, write directions on how to play a simple game—one step on each strip of paper. Mix up the strips of paper, and then have a partner put them in the correct order. Was your partner right?
- Create steps in a process for a routine you follow sometime during the day. For example, write steps for what you do when you get ready for bed at night. You might put on your pajamas first, and then brush your teeth, and so on.

WORDS! | Vocabulary

Base Words

Context Clues

Antonyms

Synonyms

Prefixes

Suffixes

Dictionary

Thesaurus

Multiple-Meaning Words

Homographs

Homonyms

Homophones

Related Words

Compound Words

Let's Think About...

Vocabulary Skills and Strategies

As you read,
- look for prefixes, suffixes, or other word parts.
- look for words in the surrounding text to figure out word meaning.
- use a dictionary, a glossary, or a thesaurus to find definitions.

Vocabulary skills and strategies are tools you use to help you figure out the meanings of words. This will help you better understand what you read.

Ready to Try It?

Base Words

A base word is a word that cannot be broken down into smaller words or word parts. *Cover* and *motion* are base words.

Cover

Motion

Knowing the meaning of a base word can help you understand the meanings of longer words.

Context Clues

Read the words before and after a word that you don't know to help you make sense of it.

I couldn't decide what to wear! The red, blue, green, or fuchsia dress?

Envision It! | Words to Know

adorable

iguana

trophies

compassionate

exactly

mature

mention

Vocabulary Strategy for

🎯 Unfamiliar Words

Context Clues What do you do when you come across an unfamiliar word? Sometimes you can figure out what the word means by looking at the words and sentences around the word. They might have clues to help you figure out the meaning of the word.

1. Read the words and sentences around the word you don't know. Sometimes the author tells you what the word means.

2. If not, use the words and sentences to predict a meaning for the word.

3. Try that meaning in the sentence. Does it make sense?

Read "Choosing a Pet" on page 121. Use context clues to help you understand the meanings of the *Words to Know* or other unfamiliar words.

Words to Write Reread "Choosing a Pet." Write about a pet you would like to have. Explain what your reasons are for choosing that pet. Use words from the *Words to Know* list in your paragraph.

Choosing a Pet

Do you want a new pet? Some people want a pet that they think is adorable. They might want a tiny kitten or a puppy. Others may want a pet that is a little different, such as an iguana or a tarantula. I've heard that there are those who just like to have a whole tank full of fish. Do you know what you want?

Maybe you want a mature animal that won't have to be trained. Maybe you want to have an animal that you can take to competitions. Would you like to win trophies? Or perhaps you want to be compassionate and rescue a pet from a shelter.

Did I mention that you should learn about your pet? It's important to be sensitive to the needs of this new member of your family. What kind of care will your new pet need? What will you feed your pet? Most animals don't eat spaghetti! Find out what you need to do to keep your pet healthy.

Choosing exactly the right pet is important. Your new pet can bring you years of happiness.

Your Turn!

Need a Review?
For additional help with context clues, see page 119.

Ready to Try It? As you read other text, use what you've learned about context clues to help you figure out the meanings of unfamiliar words.

Envision It! | **Words to Know**

bill

goo

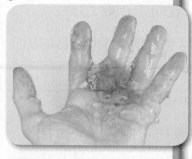

tons

hunters
material
platform
twigs

READING STREET ONLINE
VOCABULARY ACTIVITIES
www.ReadingStreet.com

Vocabulary Strategy for

Unfamiliar Words

Context Clues If you come to an unfamiliar word, look at the words around it. Context clues, or the nearby words and sentences, can help you find the meaning of an unfamiliar word. Writers often give an example, a definition, or an explanation of a word you may not know.

1. Read the words and sentences around the word you don't know. Sometimes the author tells you what the word means in the context around a word.

2. If not, use the words and sentences to predict a meaning for the word.

3. Try that meaning in the sentence to see if it makes sense.

Read "Home Tweet Home" on page 123. Use context clues to find the meanings of unfamiliar words.

Words to Write Reread "Home Tweet Home." Make a list of the *Words to Know* and any unfamiliar words in alphabetical order. Beside each word, write the context clue that helped you understand its meaning.

Home ^{Tweet} Home

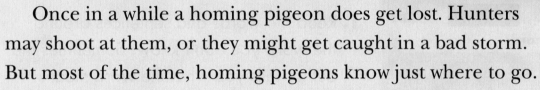

A homing pigeon is a kind of bird. It may look like other kinds of birds—with wings, a bill or beak, and feathers—but it can do something very special. A homing pigeon can find its way home from a drop-off point very far away.

Once in a while a homing pigeon does get lost. Hunters may shoot at them, or they might get caught in a bad storm. But most of the time, homing pigeons know just where to go.

Many people like to train homing pigeons. They keep their birds in their yard or on top of a roof. They may build a home with a platform where the birds can take off and land. Inside the home, the birds sleep on grass, twigs, and other kinds of material. The people must keep the pigeon's home clean, free of dirt, and other kinds of goo.

Did you know that pigeons can be used to send messages? In France, there is a statue in honor of the pigeons used during World War I. It is a large statue that weighs several tons. It shows that pigeons carried messages that helped save the lives of many people.

Your Turn!

❙❙ Need a Review?
For additional help with context clues, see page 119.

▶ Ready to Try It? As you read other text, use what you've learned about context clues to help you figure out the meanings of unfamiliar words.

Vocabulary Strategy for

Unfamiliar Words

Context Clues Sometimes when you are reading, you come across an unfamiliar word. How can you figure out what the word means? Look for context clues. Context clues are in the words and sentences around the unfamiliar word. They can help you figure out the meaning of the word.

1. Read the words and sentences around the word you don't know. Sometimes the author tells you what the word means.

2. If not, use the words and sentences to predict a meaning for the word.

3. Then try that meaning in the sentence. Does it make sense?

Read "Breaking the Ice" on page 125. Use context clues to help you understand the meanings of the *Words to Know* and other unfamiliar words.

Words to Write Look at the pictures in the *Words to Know* list and on page 125. Choose a picture to write about. Use words from the *Words to Know* list in your description.

Breaking the Ice

Josh is a sailor on a Canadian icebreaker. An icebreaker is a ship with a heavy steel bow, or front, that it uses to break through ice. Sometimes a ship, surrounded on all sides by ice, becomes trapped and can't move. The icebreaker cuts a channel through the ice so that the ship can sail to safety.

Josh likes helping people. One winter, a waterfront village on a bay in the far north had been buried by blizzards. The people were running out of food and other supplies. No one could get to the village over land, so the villagers called the icebreaker for help.

The ship had to cut a path through the ice on the bay. The people were nervous and watched the ship anxiously. They chipped away the ice around the dock so that the ship could get close enough to unload the supplies. As the ship sailed away, the villagers began to sing a song. Josh did not know the melody, or tune, but he enjoyed the symphony of voices saying thank you.

Your Turn!

⏸ **Need a Review?**
For additional help with context clues, see page 119.

▶ **Ready to Try It?** As you read other text, use what you've learned about context clues to help you figure out the meanings of unfamiliar words.

Envision It! | **Words to Know**

basketball

freeze

guard

disease

popular

sports

study

terrible

Vocabulary Strategy for

Unfamiliar Words

Context Clues Unfamiliar words are words you haven't seen before. Context clues in the nearby words and sentences can help you figure out the meaning of these new words. Writers often define or explain unfamiliar words in context to help you understand what you are reading.

1. Read the words and sentences around the word you don't know. Sometimes the author tells you what the word means.

2. If not, use the words and sentences to predict a meaning for the word.

3. Try that meaning in the sentence. Does it make sense?

Read "Carlos Catches Sports Fever" on page 127. Use context clues to help you understand the meanings of the *Words to Know*.

Words to Write Reread "Carlos Catches Sports Fever." Do you have a sport you like to play or watch? Write about the sport you are interested in. Use as many words from the *Words to Know* list as you can.

Carlos Catches Sports Fever

Ever since his parents could remember, Carlos had been a sports fanatic. He would study about his favorite players, especially basketball's most popular player: Michael Jordan. Carlos was hoping to become the greatest point guard in the history of the sport. He spent hours practicing shooting hoops in his driveway. Carlos's uncle had installed a pole, basketball hoop, and backboard so that Carlos could play all the time.

Carlos practiced in all kinds of weather, even in January. Carlos just put on extra layers of clothing and extra socks so his toes wouldn't freeze. His mother kept telling him to come inside before he caught a terrible cold. But Carlos didn't want to stop playing. He knew that Michael Jordan had become the best basketball player in history because he was so dedicated to the game. Like Michael Jordan, Carlos had the basketball "disease," but he didn't want a cure!

Your Turn!

⏸ **Need a Review?**
For additional help with context clues, see page 119.

▶ **Ready to Try It?** As you read other text, use what you've learned about context clues to help you figure out the meanings of unfamiliar words.

Envision It! Words to Know

bakery

batch

dough

boils
braided
ingredients
mixture

READING STREET ONLINE
VOCABULARY ACTIVITIES
www.ReadingStreet.com

Vocabulary Strategy for

🎯 Unfamiliar Words

Context Clues Sometimes you come across an unfamiliar word. How can you figure out what the word means? Look at the context, or the words and sentences around the word. You might find clues that can help you figure out the meaning of the word.

1. Read the words and sentences around the word you don't know. Sometimes the author tells you what the word means.

2. If not, use the words and sentences to predict a meaning for the word.

3. Try that meaning in the sentence. Does it make sense?

Read "Biscuits for Breakfast" on page 129. As you read, use context clues to help you understand the meanings of the *Words to Know* and other unfamiliar words.

Words to Write Reread "Biscuits for Breakfast." Write the directions explaining how to make your favorite breakfast food. Be sure to include the ingredients and the steps. Use words from the *Words to Know* list.

Biscuits for Breakfast

Would you like something for breakfast that you will not find in a bakery? Make biscuits! You'll need only a few ingredients to make one batch.

¾ cup shortening

1 ¾ cups flour

2 ½ teaspoons baking powder

¾ teaspoon salt

¾ cup milk

Use a fork to add the shortening to the flour, baking powder, and salt. The mixture should look like fine crumbs. Add enough milk so that the dough rounds into a ball. Put the dough on a floured board. Knead it 10 times and only 10 times.

Roll the dough flat, about ½ inch thick. Cut out round circles using a biscuit cutter or an overturned glass. Place the circles on a baking sheet. Do not let the circles touch one another. Bake at 350° for 10 to 12 minutes or until the biscuits are light brown on top. Serve them with butter and honey.

Forget about braided coffee cakes. When the water boils for your morning tea and you are looking for something to go with it, grab a hot, fresh biscuit.

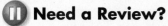

Your Turn!

❚❚ Need a Review? For additional help with context clues, see page 119.

▶ Ready to Try It? As you read other text, use what you've learned about context clues to help you figure out the meanings of unfamiliar words.

Antonyms

Antonyms are words that have opposite meanings. *Same* and *different* are antonyms.

Same

Different

Antonyms can be used to contrast two things. Antonyms help readers understand differences.

Synonyms

Synonyms are words that have the same meaning or similar meanings. *Loud* and *noisy* are synonyms.

Loud

Knowing and using synonyms can help make your writing more interesting. Look in a thesaurus to find synonyms.

Noisy

Envision It! | Words to Know

hatch

pecks

preen

cuddles

flippers

frozen

snuggles

Vocabulary Strategy for

Synonyms

Context Clues Sometimes when you are reading, you come across a word you don't know. The author may give you a synonym in the context of the word. A synonym is a word that has the same or almost the same meaning as another word. Look for a nearby word that might be a synonym to help you understand the meaning of the word you don't know.

1. Look at the words very near the word you don't know. The author may give a synonym in the sentence.

2. If not, look in the sentences around the sentence with the unfamiliar word for a synonym.

3. Try the synonym in place of the word in the sentence. Does it make sense?

Read "Penguins Are Birds" on page 133. Look for synonyms to help you understand the meanings of the vocabulary words.

Words to Write Look at the pictures in the *Words to Know* list and on page 133. Choose a picture to write about. Use words from the *Words to Know* list and synonyms in your writing.

Penguins Are Birds

All birds come from eggs. The mother bird lays the eggs, and then the mother bird or the father bird sits on the eggs until it is time for them to hatch. Each baby bird pecks, or hits, the shell of its egg with its beak until the shell breaks open. The baby bird cannot fly or get food. It needs its parents to bring it food and keep it warm. When a parent bird sits on the nest, the baby bird snuggles, or presses, into the parent's belly. The parents preen their own feathers. Then they also brush the baby bird's soft feathers. This helps keep the baby bird warm.

Penguins are birds. They have flippers instead of wings, and they swim rather than fly. But they have feathers and lay eggs just as other birds do. Baby penguins hatch from eggs, and they need their parents to give them food and warmth. Some penguins live in Antarctica, where the land and much of the water around it are frozen. Penguins don't have nests, so a penguin parent cuddles, or hugs, the egg or the chick to keep it warm.

Your Turn!

Need a Review?
For additional help with synonyms, see page 131.

Ready to Try It?
As you read other text, use what you've learned about synonyms to help you understand it.

133

Objectives
● Use context clues to figure out words you don't know or words that have more than one meaning.
● Identify words that are opposites.

Envision It! | Words to Know

bottom

crops

partners

cheated
clever
lazy
wealth

READING STREET ONLINE
VOCABULARY ACTIVITIES
www.ReadingStreet.com

Vocabulary Strategy for

Antonyms

Context Clues Sometimes you read a word you don't know. The author may give you an antonym for the word. An antonym is a word that means the opposite of a word. For example, *empty* is the opposite of *full*. Look for a word in the words or sentences nearby that might be an antonym to help you understand the word you don't know.

1. Look at the words and sentences around the word you don't know. The author may have used an antonym.

2. Find a word that seems to mean the opposite of the word you don't know.

3. Use that word to help you figure out the word you don't know.

Read "Farming" on page 135. Look for antonyms to help you understand the meanings of the *Words to Know* and other words you don't know.

Words to Write Reread "Farming." Would you like to be a farmer? Why or why not? Write about your ideas. Use words from the *Words to Know* list in your writing.

Farming

Farming is not an occupation for lazy people. Farmers are always busy. In the spring they till, or turn up, the soil to prepare it for planting. Then they dig holes, put the seeds in the bottom of each hole, and cover them with soil. In the summer, farmers water and weed the growing crops. In the fall, it is time for harvesting. Then they cut or dig up the crops in the fields. In some countries, farmers use machines to do these things. In many countries, however, farmers still do many jobs by hand.

The weather can make any farmer look clever or foolish. Too much rain and the crops wash away; not enough rain and the crops die. The weather has often cheated farmers and ruined their crops. So farmers must be partners with the weather.

Most farmers do not make a lot of money. So why do they farm? Some farm to get the food they need. Many choose to be farmers because to them wealth is not as important as working with the land.

Your Turn!

❚❚ Need a Review?
For additional help with antonyms, see page 130.

▷ Ready to Try It?
As you read other text, use what you've learned about antonyms to help you understand it.

Objectives
● Use context clues to figure out words you don't know or words that have more than one meaning.
● Identify words that have similar meanings.

Envision It! | **Words to Know**

festival

handkerchief

snug

cotton
graceful
paces
pale
rhythm

Vocabulary Strategy for

🎯 Synonyms

Context Clues Sometimes, you might read a word you don't know. The author may have used a synonym that gives you a clue to the meaning of the unknown word. A synonym is a word that has the same or almost the same meaning as another word. For example, *difficult* is a synonym for *hard*.

1. Look at the words and sentences near the unknown word. The author may have used a synonym.

2. Do you recognize a word that might be a synonym?

3. Use the synonym in place of the unknown word. Does it make sense?

Read "Pass It Down" on page 137. Use synonyms to help you understand the meanings of unknown words.

Words to Write Reread "Pass It Down." Recall a story about someone in your family. Write it down or make one up. Use words from the *Words to Know* list and synonyms in your story.

Pass It Down

Emily Douglas is named after her grandmother, Emily Kelly. Every summer Emily Kelly's village in Ireland held a dance festival and contest. Emily K. was eight the first time she entered the contest. She had practiced for weeks, but she was very nervous and started to worry. One shoe felt comfortably snug while the other felt too tight. When the fiddles began playing, her heart was thumping so loudly that she couldn't hear the rhythm. So she started a few paces, or steps, behind the beat. That's the way she did the entire dance!

When she finished, everyone applauded and cheered. The judges told her how graceful she was and how original her dance was! She won first prize—a pale blue cotton handkerchief embroidered with white flowers. When Emily K. came to the United States, the handkerchief was one of the few things she brought with her. Later she gave it to her granddaughter, Emily. Emily has kept the handkerchief. It makes her think about another girl named Emily.

Your Turn!

❙❙ Need a Review?
For additional help with synonyms, see page 131.

▶ Ready to Try It? As you read other text, use what you've learned about synonyms to help you understand it.

Objectives
● Use context clues to figure out words you don't know or words that have more than one meaning.
● Identify words that are opposites.

Envision It! | Words to Know

foreign

narrow

recipe

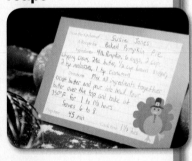

bows

chilly

foolish

perches

READING STREET ONLINE
VOCABULARY ACTIVITIES
www.ReadingStreet.com

Vocabulary Strategy for

🎯 Antonyms

Context Clues Sometimes you will read a word you don't know. The author may include an antonym for the word. An antonym is a word that means the opposite of another word. For example, *hot* is the opposite of *cold*. Look for an antonym to figure out the meaning of the word.

1. Look at the words around the unfamiliar word. The author may have used an antonym.

2. Do you recognize a word that seems to have opposite meaning of the unfamiliar word?

3. Use the antonym to help you figure out the meaning of the unfamiliar word.

Read "Mr. Wang's Wonderful Noodles" on page 139. Look for antonyms to help you understand the meanings of unfamiliar words.

Words to Write Reread "Mr. Wang's Wonderful Noodles." Write about your favorite food. How does it taste? Why do you like it? Use words from the *Words to Know* list and antonyms in your story.

MR. WANG'S WONDERFUL Noodles

Mr. Wang is the best noodle maker in Shanghai, China. People who like wide, thick noodles may think people who like narrow, thin noodles are foolish. People who like narrow, thin noodles may think people who like wide, thick noodles are not very smart. But everyone agrees on one thing. Mr. Wang's noodles are the best.

One day, a stranger perches on a stool at the noodle shop. Mr. Wang bows his head in respect. The stranger says, "Mr. Wang, please bring your noodle recipe to the United States. Make noodles in my restaurant."

People stop slurping their noodles to listen to Mr. Wang's reply. The warm shop suddenly feels chilly.

Mr. Wang says, "Thank you. But I do not wish to go to a foreign land. I am happy making noodles in China."

Everyone heaves a sigh of relief. Everyone goes back to slurping Mr. Wang's wonderful noodles.

Your Turn!

❚❚ Need a Review?
For additional help with antonyms, see page 130.

▶ Ready to Try It?
As you read other text, use what you've learned about antonyms to help you understand it.

Prefixes

A prefix is a word part that can be added to the beginning of a base word. In the word *uncover, un-* is a prefix.

Cover

Uncover

Knowing the meaning of a prefix can help you figure out the meaning of a new word.

Common Prefixes and Their Meanings

un-	not
re-	again, back
in-	not
dis-	not, opposite of
pre-	before

140

Suffixes

A suffix is a word part added to the end of a base word. In the word *motionless*, *-less* is a suffix.

Motion

Motionless

Common Suffixes and Their Meanings

-able	can be done
-ment	action or process
-less	without
-tion	act, process

Knowing how a suffix changes a word can help you figure out the meaning of a new word.

Objectives

● Understand the meaning of common prefixes and common suffixes, and understand how they affect the root word.

arranged

bundles

unwrapped

errands

excitedly

dangerously

steady

wobbled

Vocabulary Strategy for

Prefixes and Suffixes

Word Structure When you read a word you don't know, see if it has a prefix or suffix. A prefix is a word part added in front of a base word to form a new word. The prefix *un-* makes a word mean "not ____ " or "the opposite of ____, " as in *unhappy*: "not happy." A suffix is a word part added to the end of a base word to form a new word. The suffix *-ly* makes a word mean "in a ____ way" as in *slowly*: "in a slow way."

1. Put your finger over the prefix or suffix.

2. Look at the base word, the part of the word without the suffix. Put the base word in the phrase "the opposite of ____" or "in a ____ way."

3. Try that meaning in the sentence. Does it make sense?

As you read "A Gift for Cletus," look for words that begin with *un-* or end with *-ly*. Use the prefix or suffix to help you figure out the meanings of the words.

Words to Write Reread "A Gift for Cletus." What do you think Cletus should save his money for now? Write your ideas. Use words from the *Words to Know* list.

A GIFT FOR CLETUS

Every Saturday Cletus ran errands for his neighbors to earn money. They gave him lists of things to buy in town. They gave him bundles to drop off. Sometimes Cletus had so much piled on the front of his bike that he could not keep the bike steady. He wobbled dangerously from side to side, and the bundles would almost fall into the street. Cletus had to ride very slowly, keeping one hand on the bundles.

Cletus wanted to buy a big basket for the back of his bike. He knew that with the bundles arranged behind him, it would be easier and safer to ride back and forth to town. But he had been unable to save enough money.

The neighbors really appreciated what Cletus did for them. They wanted a way to say thank you. So they got together and bought Cletus a basket for his bike. He unwrapped the gift and excitedly put the new basket on his bike. He thanked his neighbors, and then off he went again with their lists and bundles.

Your Turn!

Need a Review?
For additional help with prefixes and suffixes, see pages 140–141.

Ready to Try It? As you read other text, use what you've learned about prefixes and suffixes to help you understand it.

search

stinging

survivors

incredible	topic
lofty	unseen
noble	waterless

Vocabulary Strategy for

🎯 Prefixes and Suffixes

Word Structure When you see a word you don't know, look closely at it. Does it have a prefix at the beginning or a suffix at the end? The prefix *un-* makes a word mean "not _____" or "the opposite of _____." For example, *unhappy* means "not happy." The suffix *-ing* tells that the verb is an ongoing action, such as *running,* or turns a verb into an adjective, as in *"running* shoes."

1. Does the word you don't know have a prefix or a suffix? If so, put your finger on it.

2. Look at the base word. Do you know what the base word means?

3. Now use the prefix or suffix to figure out the meaning of the whole word.

4. Try your meaning in the sentence. Does it make sense?

Read "A Trip to Death Valley" on page 145. Look for words with prefixes or suffixes, and use them to figure out the words' meanings.

Words to Write Reread "A Trip to Death Valley." Write a short paragraph about life in the desert. Use words with prefixes and suffixes and from the *Words to Know* list.

A Trip to Death Valley

Have you ever been to the desert? It is an incredible place. Some people like to go hiking in Death Valley National Park in the spring. Before they go, they need to know how to be survivors in this noble, waterless land.

Hikers need to make sure they have plenty of water. They should wear cool, loose fitting clothing. Good hiking boots are a must.

It is probably best to go with a guide. The guide will know all about the topic of desert life. Park rangers take tour groups to see some wonderful desert sights.

Desert travelers will want to search for unseen animals among the Joshua trees and sand dunes. Will they see a stinging scorpion? There may be a coyote or a bobcat nearby. There are some man-made sights too. A lofty thermometer sits 135 feet high near the desert town of Baker, California!

If you decide to go on a desert adventure, don't go unprepared! You will see a very special place.

Your Turn!

Need a Review? For additional help with prefixes and suffixes, see pages 140–141.

Ready to Try It? As you read other text, use what you've learned about prefixes and suffixes to help you understand it.

Envision It! Words to Know

crown

liberty

torch

models

symbol

tablet

unforgettable

unveiled

Vocabulary Strategy for

🎯 Prefix *un-*

Word Structure Prefixes can give you clues to the meanings of unfamiliar words. The prefix *un-* at the beginning of a word means "not ____." For example, *un*pleasant means "not pleasant." When *un-* is added to a verb, it usually means the reverse of the verb. For instance, *un*cover means "to remove a cover."

1. When you see an unfamiliar word with a prefix, cover up the prefix.

2. What does the base word mean without the prefix?

3. Add *not* in front of the word. Does this meaning make sense in the sentence?

Read "Emma and Liberty" on page 147. Look for words that have prefixes. Use your knowledge of prefixes to find the meanings of these words.

Words to Write Reread "Emma and Liberty." What symbols of freedom have you seen or heard about? Write about symbols of freedom. Use as many words from the *Words to Know* list as you can.

Emma and Liberty

Emma is visiting New York City. What she wants to see more than anything else is the remarkable Statue of Liberty. Emma knows everything about Liberty. She knows why the statue was made, who made it, and when it was unveiled. She knows how tall it is from its base to its crown, what its torch is made of, and what is written on the tablet. Emma has collected pictures of the statue and reproduced models of it. However, she has never seen the real Liberty.

From Battery Park in Lower Manhattan, Emma has a breathless view of the Statue of Liberty in the distance. She waits in line for the boat that will safely take her to Liberty Island. As the boat gets nearer, Emma imagines what it was like for the immigrants who sailed past Liberty as they arrived in America.

At last Emma is standing at Liberty's feet. She tilts her head back to look up at this symbol of freedom. It is an unforgettable moment.

Your Turn!

❚❚ Need a Review?
For additional help with prefixes, see page 140.

▶ Ready to Try It? As you read other text, use what you've learned about prefixes to help you understand it.

crystal

discovery

scoop

disappeared
goal
journey
joyful
unaware

148

Vocabulary Strategy for

Prefixes and Suffixes
un-, dis-, and *-ful*

Word Structure When you see a word you don't know, look for a prefix or suffix. The prefixes *un-* or *dis-* make a word mean "not ____" or "opposite of ____." The suffix *-ful* makes a word mean "full of ____." Use *un-, dis-,* or *-ful* to figure out the meanings of words.

1. When you see an unfamiliar word with a prefix or suffix, put your finger over the prefix or suffix.

2. Look at the base word. Put the base word in the appropriate phrase: "not____, " "opposite of ____," or "full of ____."

3. Try the new meaning in the sentence. Does it make sense?

Read "How Ants Find Food" on page 149. Look for words that have a prefix or suffix. Use the prefix or suffix to help you figure out the meanings of the words.

Words to Write Reread "How Ants Find Food." Write about the jobs a worker ant does. Use words from the *Words to Know* list in your writing.

How Ants Find Food

Ants are social insects. Like wasps and bees, they live in large groups called colonies. The queen ant lays all the eggs, and the worker ants build the nest, look for food, care for the eggs, and defend the nest.

Ants that look for food are called scouts. Their goal is to find food and report the locations to the ants back at the nest. Suppose a scout ant makes this discovery: someone has left out a scoop of sugar. The scout carries a sugar crystal back to the nest. On its return journey, the scout ant also leaves a scent trail leading from the food to the nest. When the other ants realize that the scout has found food, they become very excited. They seem joyful about the news.

Many ants follow the scout's trail back to the food. They swarm over the sugar, picking up all the crystals. In a short time, all of the sugar has disappeared, and so have the ants. It happens so quickly that often people are unaware that ants were ever there at all.

Your Turn!

❚❚ Need a Review?
For additional help with prefixes and suffixes, see pages 140–141.

▶ Ready to Try It? As you read other text, use what you've learned about prefixes and suffixes to help you understand it.

Dictionary

A dictionary is a book that explains the words of our language. The words in a dictionary are in alphabetical order.

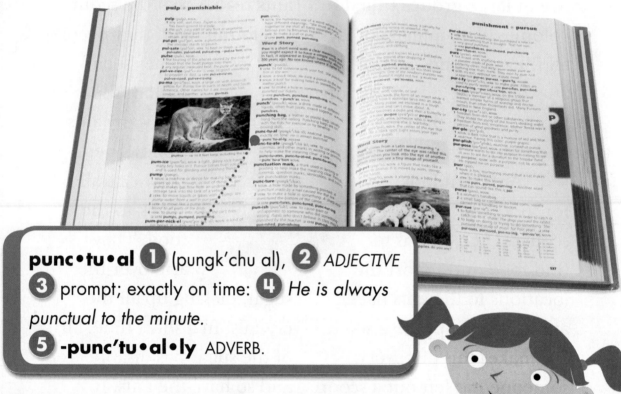

punc•tu•al ❶ (pungk'chu al), ❷ *ADJECTIVE*
❸ prompt; exactly on time: ❹ *He is always punctual to the minute.*
❺ **-punc'tu•al•ly** ADVERB.

❶ This part of the entry shows you how to pronounce the word.

❷ The dictionary entry tells you the word's part of speech. *Punctual* is an adjective.

❸ Here is the word's definition.

❹ The word is used in an example to help you understand its meaning.

❺ See how the word changes when it has a suffix added.

Thesaurus

A thesaurus is a book of synonyms. The words in a thesaurus are in alphabetical order.

cute
adjective
attractive, appealing, amusing, charming, adorable, enchanting

Keep a thesaurus handy when you write. It can help you find just the right word.

Spot is so cute!

Envision It! | Words to Know

gear

parka

willow

splendid

twitch

yanked

Vocabulary Strategy for

🎯 Unknown Words

Dictionary/Glossary You can use a glossary or a dictionary to find the meaning of an unknown word. A glossary appears at the back of a book. It defines important words from that book. A dictionary is a book that lists words, their meanings, and other information about the words. Glossaries and dictionaries list words in alphabetical order.

1. Look at the first letter in the word.

2. Turn to the section in the glossary or dictionary for that letter to find the entry.

3. If the word has more than one meaning, decide which meaning fits the sentence.

4. Try that meaning in the sentence to see if it makes sense.

Read "First Snow" on page 153. As you read, make a list of the highlighted words. Use a glossary or a dictionary to find the meaning of each word and write it next to the word.

Words to Write Reread "First Snow." What do you think Jack and Missy missed most about Florida? Write your ideas. Use words from the *Words to Know* list.

First Snow

Jack and Missy had never seen snow. They lived in Florida. The weather there was too warm for snow. Then last winter they visited their cousins in Michigan.

On the second day of their visit, a snowstorm brought seven inches of the splendid white stuff. Hooray! Jack and Missy borrowed their cousins' extra boots and other outdoor gear. Then they all ran outside to play.

In the yard, the willow trees looked like they were made of snow. All the branches were covered in white. Missy went closer for a better look. Just then Jack yanked one of the branches. The snow poured down onto Missy's head. Some fell inside the neck of her parka. Brrr! The cold made her twitch and shiver, but she laughed anyway.

They took turns pulling each other in the sled. They made a snowman. Finally they were too cold and wet to stay outside. They went inside for dry clothes.

Jack and Missy had fun playing in the snow all week. By the end of the visit, though, they were glad to go back to the sunshine of Florida.

Your Turn!

Need a Review?
For additional help with using a dictionary, see page 150.

Ready to Try It? As you read other text, use a dictionary or glossary to help you find the meanings of unknown words.

Envision It! | Words to Know

antlers

languages

poked

imagined

narrator

overhead

Vocabulary Strategy for

🎯 Unknown Words

Dictionary/Glossary If you read a word you don't know, you can look it up in a dictionary or a glossary to find the correct meaning, how the word is divided into syllables, which syllables are stressed, and how to pronounce the word correctly.

1. Look up the word in a dictionary. Entries are in alphabetical order.

2. Use the pronunciation key and look at each syllable to pronounce the word.

3. Read all the meanings of the word. Then choose the one that makes the best sense in the sentence.

Read "The Class Play" on page 155. Use a dictionary or a glossary to find the meanings and pronunciations of the *Words to Know*.

Words to Write Reread "The Class Play." Imagine you are Ms. Chavez. What would you say to Jenna and Kate? Write your response. Use words from the *Words to Know* list.

The Class Play

"I have counted the votes," declared Ms. Chavez, waving a sheet of paper overhead. "Our play for Parents Night will be *Pushing Up the Sky*. Tryouts are tomorrow."

Jenna grinned and poked Kate in the shoulder. They both wanted to be Chiefs together. They had already learned the lines and planned their costumes.

The next day, Jenna tried out for the First Chief. That was scarier than she had imagined. She forgot several words.

When Kate tried out for the Seventh Chief's part, she didn't make a single mistake.

Later, Ms. Chavez announced the parts. Kate was the Narrator. She had a lot of lines, but she didn't get to wear a costume. "But I made such a beautiful cape," she wailed.

Jenna was the Elk. She didn't have any lines at all, and she had to wear brown paper antlers on her head. "Don't elks know *any* languages?"

Both girls were disappointed but glad to be in the play. Maybe next time they would get the parts they wanted.

Your Turn!

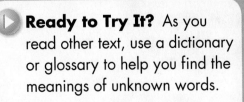

❚❚ Need a Review?
For additional help with using a dictionary, see page 150.

▷ Ready to Try It? As you read other text, use a dictionary or glossary to help you find the meanings of unknown words.

Envision It! | Words to Know

ladle

patterns

temperature

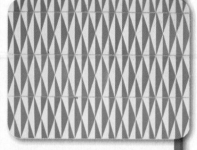

dim

gas

gigantic

shine

Vocabulary Strategy for

🎯 Unknown Words

Dictionary/Glossary When you read an unknown word, a glossary or an electronic dictionary can help you find out its meaning. A dictionary also gives you other information, such as the number of syllables, which syllables are stressed, parts of speech, history, and pronunciation of the word.

1. Look up the word in a dictionary.

2. Use the pronunciation key, the syllable divisions, and stressed syllables to pronounce the word correctly.

3. Read the meanings for the word.

4. Choose the meaning that seems the best. Does it make sense in the sentence?

Read "A Letter from Far Away" on page 157. Use an electronic dictionary to find the meanings and pronunciations of the *Words to Know*.

Words to Write Reread "A Letter from Far Away." Write a letter to a friend about a real or an imaginary trip. Use words from the *Words to Know* list in your letter.

A Letter from Far Away

Dear Mom and Dad,

Grandpa and I are having a great time on our camping trip. We set up our tent right by the lake. I caught two fish today! The weather has been really hot. I hope the temperature goes down soon.

It's exciting to be so far away from the city. It is really dark here at night. I love the way the stars shine so brightly. These stars are nothing like the dim little dots we see in the city. Grandpa says that each star is a huge, gigantic ball of hot gas. That's amazing!

Grandpa and I like to look for patterns in the stars. Grandpa showed me some stars that form the shape of a ladle. I thought it looked more like a yo-yo than a big old spoon!

I'll mail this letter tomorrow, when we hike into town.

Love,
Darren

Your Turn!

⏸ Need a Review? For additional help with using a dictionary, see page 150.

▶ Ready to Try It? As you read other text, use a dictionary or glossary to help you find the meanings of unknown words.

Envision It! | Words to Know

erupted

outrun

tides

average

depth

deserts

peak

waterfalls

Vocabulary Strategy for

🎯 Unknown Words

Dictionary/Glossary You can use a dictionary or glossary to find the meaning of an unknown word. The words in a dictionary or glossary are in alphabetical order.

Follow these steps with *deepest, deserts,* and *depth* from "Geography Bee."

1. Open a dictionary.

2. Look at the first three letters in the word. Put them in alphabetical order, and then find and read all entries for the word. (Remember to look up the base words of *deepest* and *deserts*.)

3. Decide which meaning you think fits in the sentence if there is more than one meaning listed.

4. Try that meaning in the sentence to see if it makes sense.

Read "Geography Bee" on page 159. Use a glossary or a dictionary to help you find the meanings of other unknown words.

Words to Write Reread "Geography Bee." Write four geography bee questions about your state. Then find and write the answers. Use words from the *Words to Know* list.

Geography Bee

Have you heard of a geography bee? You probably know what a spelling bee is. In a spelling bee, people take turns spelling difficult words. The person who spells the most words correctly wins. In a geography bee, people answer questions about places on Earth.

The questions in a geography bee will never have a yes or no answer. For example, this question would not be used in a geography bee: Can a person outrun the tides at the Bay of Fundy?

To answer the questions in a geography bee, you must know facts about continents, countries, states, and physical features of the world, such as deserts or oceans.

Here are some sample questions for you to try: When was the last time Mount St. Helen's erupted? What is the hottest spot on Earth? Which is the highest of all the waterfalls on Earth? Which mountain peak is the tallest in the world? What is the average summer temperature at the South Pole? What is the depth of the deepest point of Marianas Trench?

Your Turn!

Need a Review? For additional help with using a dictionary, see page 150.

Ready to Try It? As you read other text, use a dictionary or glossary to help you find the meanings of unknown words.

Envision It! | Words to Know

gully

reeds

valley

clutched

echoed

scrambled

thatch

Vocabulary Strategy for

⟳ Unknown Words

Dictionary/Glossary You can use a dictionary or glossary to find the meaning, syllable division, and pronunciation of an unknown word.

1. Find the entry word and pronunciation in a dictionary or glossary.

2. Look at the pronunciation key and each syllable to pronounce the word correctly.

3. Read all of the definitions. Which meaning best fits the sentence?

4. Try that meaning in the sentence. If it doesn't make sense, try another meaning of the word.

Read "Eagle Watching" on page 161. Use a dictionary or glossary to find the meanings, syllable divisions, and pronunciations of the *Words to Know*.

Words to Write Reread "Eagle Watching." What kind of animals are you interested in studying? Write about your interest. Use words from the *Words to Know* list in your answer.

Eagle Watching

José and his father scrambled up the side of the gully. Near the top of the gully was their favorite eagle-watching spot. José and his father looked for the bald eagles that lived in the area. First, they used their binoculars to scan the tops of the trees. Eagles usually perch in high places so that they can look for food. Next, José and his father listened for the eagles. Loud eagle cries often echoed across the valley.

In the valley below where José and his father hid was a large lake. The eagles swooped over the reeds and thatch along the lake's edge, skimmed over the surface, and dipped down and snatched fish out of the water. Then the eagles flew away with the fish clutched in their sharp talons, or claws. They carried the fish back to their nests, high in the tall trees or on the cliffs. It was an amazing sight, and José never got tired of watching it.

Your Turn!

⏸ **Need a Review?** For additional help with using a dictionary, see page 150.

▶ **Ready to Try It?** As you read other text, use a dictionary or glossary to help you find the meanings of unknown words.

Objectives

● Put a series of words in alphabetical order up to the third letter. ● Use a dictionary or glossary to look up the meanings, syllable patterns, and ways to say words you do not know.

Envision It! | Words to Know

encourages

expression

native

local

settled

social

support

Vocabulary Strategy for

🎯 Unknown Words

Dictionary/Glossary When you read an unknown word, ask yourself if it's a noun, verb, or adjective. Knowing what part of speech a word is can help you find and understand its meaning. Then use a dictionary or glossary to find the correct meaning and how the word is pronounced.

1. Use the first letter in the word to find it in the dictionary or glossary.

2. Look at the pronunciation key and each syllable to pronounce the word correctly.

3. Read the definitions of the word. Choose a meaning for the correct part of speech.

4. Try your meaning in the sentence. Does it make sense? If not, try another meaning.

Read "Class Art" on page 163. Use a dictionary or glossary to find the meanings and pronunciations of the *Words to Know*.

Words to Write Reread "Class Art." Sort the *Words to Know* into three groups: nouns, adjectives, and verbs, according to how each is used in the selection.

Class Art

Ms. Ramsey's students are excited. They are planning to paint a mural on one wall in their classroom. Ms. Ramsey encourages the students to talk about what they will paint on the mural. Everyone has a different idea. Julio's family came to the United States from Mexico. He wants to paint something about his native country. Mary wants to paint something about the community's history. Her family settled here a long, long time ago. Gerrard thinks the mural should show the social life of the people who live in the community. Diana thinks the mural should be more about global, not local, issues. It should show how the community is part of the world. How can the students get all these ideas on one mural? Ms. Ramsey points out that the mural should be an expression of the group's interests and beliefs. She says that with a little planning, the students can paint a mural that will support everyone's ideas.

Your Turn!

Need a Review? For additional help with using a dictionary, see page 150.

Ready to Try It? As you read other text, use a dictionary or glossary to help you find the meanings of unknown words.

Multiple-Meaning Words

Multiple-meaning words are words that can have different meanings depending on how they are used.

Homographs

Homographs are words that are spelled the same but have different meanings. They may be pronounced the same way or differently.

Lead

Lead

Read the words before and after a homograph to discover its meaning and pronunciation. Check a dictionary to be sure.

Homonyms

Homonyms are words that are spelled the same and sound the same, but they have different meanings.

Seal

Seal

You can figure out the meaning of a homonym by reading the words around it.

Homophones

Homophones are words that sound the same, but they are spelled differently and they have different meanings.

Hair

Hare

Homophones might be confusing when *you* hear them being read aloud. Pay attention to the words before and after the homophone to find its meaning.

Understanding
Homographs, Homonyms, and Homophones

	Pronunciation	Spelling	Meaning
Homographs	may be the same or different	same	different
Homonyms	same	same	different
Homophones	same	different	different

Homographs

tear

tear

John

ear

Homonyms

ear

berry

Homophones

bury

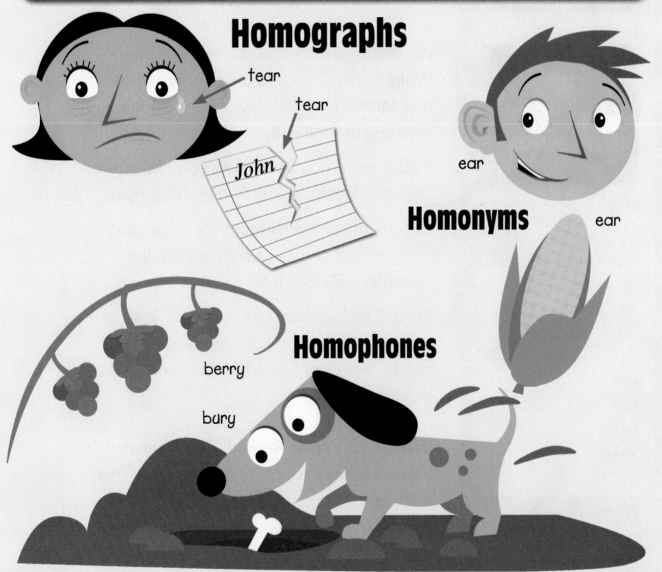

bat

battery

plug

blew

fuel

term

vision

Vocabulary Strategy for
🎯 Homonyms

Context Clues Sometimes when you are reading, you may come to a word you know, but it doesn't make sense in the sentence. The word might be a homograph. Homographs are words that are spelled the same but have different meanings. They may or may not be pronounced the same. When homographs are pronounced the same, they are also called homonyms. For example, *bat* can mean "a stick used to hit a ball" or "a flying animal." Look at the nearby words and sentences to help you figure out the meaning of a homonym.

1. If a word you know doesn't make sense in the sentence, it may be a homonym.

2. Look at the words around it. Can you figure out another meaning from the sentence? Does it make sense?

Read "The Inventor." As you read, look for words that might be homonyms. Look for nearby words to figure out the meaning that makes sense.

Words to Write Reread "The Inventor." Make a list of the homonyms you find. Then write both meanings of each word. Write sentences using each meaning of the words.

The Inventor

Max liked to invent things. He spent a lot of time working on projects in his lab. His neighbors admired his vision and creativity, but their children thought he was strange. They told each other that he kept a bat as a pet. They stayed out of his yard.

One hot summer day, Max had a terrific idea. He wanted to create something the children would enjoy. It would not need a battery. It would not plug into the wall or use fuel such as gasoline. Max's invention would run on a special kind of power—kid power!

Max wanted to use the invention soon, so he set a short term for the project. He worked day and night to finish. When the amazing "Summer Splasher" was ready, Max set it up in his front yard. Some children stopped to ask Max what it was. He showed them how to jump on the big pedal to pump water through the sprinkler. This also made the fan move. A cool breeze blew across the yard. Soon the children were lining up to try it out.

Your Turn!

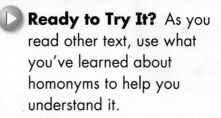

❙❙ Need a Review?
For additional help with homonyms, see page 165.

▶ Ready to Try It? As you read other text, use what you've learned about homonyms to help you understand it.

Envision It! | Words to Know

laundry

section

shelves

spoiled
store
thousands
traded
variety

Vocabulary Strategy for

⦿ Multiple-Meaning Words

Context Clues Multiple-meaning words are words that have more than one meaning. Use context clues, or nearby words and sentences, to help you figure out the correct meaning of the word.

1. When you see a word you know but the meaning doesn't make sense, it may be a multiple-meaning word.

2. Use nearby words and sentences to figure out the correct meaning of the multiple-meaning word.

3. Try the new meaning in the sentence. Does it make sense?

Read "The Library" on page 171. Look for multiple-meaning words. Try the different meanings of the words in context. See which makes sense in the sentence.

Words to Write Reread "The Library." Write about a trip to the library. Tell how you would choose some special books. Use words from the *Words to Know* list.

The Library

Martita was cleaning her room. She picked up her dirty clothes and put them into the basket with the other laundry. "Let's finish our chores," her mother said. "We'll go to the library as soon as you're done."

Now Martita was eager to finish. She put her books on the shelves. Under the bed she found a variety of puzzle pieces and magazines. In the kitchen, Martita washed the dishes left from breakfast. Then she put the milk away so that it would not get spoiled. "I'm done!" she called to her mother. "Let's go!"

They stopped at the grocery store first. Martita chose the vegetables they'd cook for dinner that night.

"You've been helping so much with the chores," her mother said. "Today you can check out two books from the library instead of one."

This made Martita feel proud. At the library, she headed for the children's section. She picked a book and read the back cover. Then she traded it for another one. There were thousands of books to choose from! But she finally chose the two she wanted. "If I clean my room every day, can I check out three books next time?" she asked her mother.

Your Turn!

Need a Review? For additional help with multiple-meaning words, see pages 164–167.

Ready to Try It? As you read other text, use what you've learned about multiple-meaning words to help you understand it.

171

Objectives

● Identify words that are opposites, words that are similar, words that have more than one meaning, and words that sound the same even though they mean different things.

area

grapevine

raisin

artificial

preservative

proof

raise

Vocabulary Strategy for

🎯 Homophones

Context Clues Homophones are words that sound the same but have different meanings and spellings, such as *write* (to write with a pen or pencil) and *right* (true, just, good). Context clues in the words and sentences nearby can help you figure out which meaning goes with which spelling of a homophone.

1. If a word you know doesn't make sense in the sentence, it may be a homophone.

2. Look at the words around it. Can you figure out the meaning?

3. Try the new meaning in the sentence. Does it make sense?

As you read "Baking with Aunt Millie" on page 173, look for homophones. Use context clues to help you figure out the meanings of the homophones and the *Words to Know*.

Words to Write Reread "Baking with Aunt Millie." Write about something special you like to do with a relative or a friend. Use homophones and words from the *Words to Know* list in your paragraph.

Baking with Aunt Millie ♡

I love to visit my Aunt Millie. Her house is so pretty and it always smells so good.

There is a big grapevine wreath on the front door. She decorates it with an artificial flower and a bow.

Her kitchen has a special area where Aunt Millie likes to bake. She collects recipes from many different countries. She tells me stories of when she was young. She grew up on a farm in a faraway place. I always laugh when she tells me how she used to raise chickens!

Aunt Millie is a very good cook. She does not like to use any kind of preservative in her baking. Her ingredients are always natural. She always had fresh eggs when she was a girl on the farm. She still likes to use the best eggs.

We always make special oatmeal raisin cookies when I visit. I get to measure the flour, the oatmeal, and the sugar. I stir in the eggs and the raisins. Aunt Millie lets me take a big basket of cookies home. She always says, "Now you have proof you were at your Aunt Millie's house today!"

Your Turn!

❚❚ Need a Review?
For additional help with homophones, see page 166.

▶ Ready to Try It?
As you read other text, use what you've learned about homophones to help you understand it.

chores

labeled

stamps

attic
board
customer
spare

Vocabulary Strategy for

Multiple-Meaning Words

Context Clues You may read a word you know but whose meaning does not make sense in the sentence. The word may have more than one meaning. For example, *bug* means both "an insect" and "to annoy."

1. Try the meaning of the word that you know. Does it make sense in the sentence?

2. If it does not make sense, perhaps it has another meaning. Can you figure out another meaning from the context?

3. Try the new meaning in the sentence. Does it make sense?

Read "More Than a Hobby" on page 175. Look for words that might have more than one meaning. Remember to use nearby words to figure out the correct meaning.

Words to Write Reread "More Than a Hobby." What kind of shop would you like to open? Write about your shop. Use words from the *Words to Know* list in your answer.

More Than a Hobby

It starts out as a hobby. As a child, you collect stamps or toy cars or rocks. At first, collecting is an activity you do in your spare time or after doing your chores.

Perhaps you collect a few rocks here and a few rocks there. Then one day you realize that the shelves in your room are bulging with rocks. So you move them to the basement or to the attic where there is more space.

As you get older, you learn more about rocks, and you talk with other rock collectors. You begin to think,

Maybe this isn't just a hobby. Could it be a business?

So you open a rock shop. Every rock in the shop is labeled with information about the rock and how much it costs. This really impresses your very first customer, so he buys several rocks. You are on your way.

Over time, your small business grows large, and you become the chairman of the board. And it all starts with a hobby.

Your Turn!

❚❚ Need a Review? For additional help with multiple-meaning words, see pages 164–167.

▶ Ready to Try It? As you read other text, use what you've learned about multiple-meaning words to help you understand it.

celebrate

current

medals

continued

drowned

stirred

strokes

Vocabulary Strategy for

🎯 Multiple-Meaning Words

Context Clues You may read a word that doesn't make sense in a sentence. The word may have another meaning. For example, *safe* can mean "free from harm" or "a metal box for storing money and valuables."

1. Try the meaning of the word that you know. Does it make sense in the sentence?

2. If not, perhaps the word has another meaning. Read on and look at the words around it to figure out another meaning.

3. Try the new meaning in the sentence. Does it make sense?

Read "Learn to Swim" on page 177. Look for words that can have more than one meaning. Use nearby words to figure out a new meaning.

Words to Write Reread "Learn to Swim." Think about another sport or activity you know. Write an article about it, including the rules for safety. Use words from the *Words to Know* list in your article.

LEARN TO SWIM

Some people swim for exercise, some swim in races, and some swim for fun. But no matter the reason, everyone should learn how to swim. People have drowned because they couldn't swim.

The first step is to learn to float, bob, and tread water. Then learn to swim the basic strokes—front crawl, backstroke, breaststroke, and sidestroke. These are different ways of moving through the water quickly.

Take your time when you're learning to swim. You're not trying to win medals in the Olympics. You do want to coordinate your arms, legs, and breathing.

Even after you know how to swim, never swim where there is no lifeguard. Ocean tides can pull you under, a river's current can sweep you away, and weather can cause problems too. One swimmer continued to swim after it started to rain. High winds stirred up the water. Luckily, a boater helped the swimmer back to shore.

So, celebrate the beginning of your life-long swimming adventure. Everyone into the pool!

Your Turn!

⏸ Need a Review?
For additional help with multiple-meaning words, see pages 164–167.

▶ Ready to Try It? As you read other text, use what you've learned about multiple-meaning words to help you understand it.

Envision It! | Words to Know

bouquet

circus

pier

difficult

nibbling

soars

swallow

Vocabulary Strategy for

Homophones

Context Clues You may read or hear a word you know, but the meaning doesn't make sense in the sentence. The word might be a homophone. Homophones are words that are pronounced the same but have different meanings and spellings. For example, the words *bear* and *bare* are homophones. A *bear* is "a large mammal" and *bare* means "not covered."

1. If the word you know doesn't make sense in the sentence, it might be a homophone.

2. Look at the words around it. Can you figure out another meaning?

3. Try the new meaning in the sentence. Does it make sense?

Read "Island Vacation" on page 179. Use context clues to determine the meanings of homophones.

Words to Write Reread "Island Vacation." What kind of places are you interested in traveling to? Write about your interest. Use homophones and words from the *Words to Know* list.

Island Vacation

Every summer my family goes to Cherry Island for a vacation. It is my favorite place in the whole world. Cherry Island is a small island with just a few cabins and houses. You can't drive to Cherry Island because there is no bridge. You have to take a boat.

My sisters and I play all over the island. We like to pick wildflowers and make a bouquet for our mother. We also like to pack a picnic lunch and eat it down by the water. We sit on the pier, nibbling on sandwiches. Sometimes a gull soars over us while we eat. Once my sister, Jane, threw some pieces of bread in the water. A huge crowd of gulls came and tried to eat the bread. It was like a circus, so crowded and noisy! Now I am always careful not to leave my sandwich on the pier because I know a gull might grab it and swallow it in one big bite.

At the end of our vacation, it is always difficult to say good-bye to Cherry Island. As the boat pulls away, I start counting the days until I can come back again.

Your Turn!

Need a Review?
For additional help with homophones, see page 166.

Ready to Try It? As you read other text, use what you've learned about homophones to help you understand it.

Envision It! Words to Know

cardboard

feast

treasure

fierce
flights
pitcher
ruined
stoops

Vocabulary Strategy for

🎯 Homonyms

Context Clues You may read a familiar word that doesn't make sense in the sentence. The word could be a homonym. Homonyms are words that are pronounced and spelled the same, but have different meanings. For example, *saw* means both "looked at" and "a tool for cutting." Use the context—the words and sentences around the word—to figure out the correct meaning.

1. Reread the words and sentences around the word that doesn't make sense.

2. Draw a conclusion about a meaning for the word using context clues.

3. Try the meaning in the sentence. Does it make sense?

Read "A Different Treasure Hunt" on page 181. Use context clues to help you find the meanings of homonyms.

Words to Write Reread "A Different Treasure Hunt." Write your answer to the question at the end of the selection. Give reasons for your answer. Use homonyms and words from the *Words to Know* list in your answer.

A DIFFERENT TREASURE HUNT

The summer I turned eight, my family moved from New York City to North Carolina. In the city, we climbed four flights of stairs to our apartment. The building was ten stories high! People sat on their front stoops and listened to the noise. I was a pitcher on the neighborhood baseball team.

In North Carolina, we live in a house. All the houses have front porches and yards. At night it is very dark and quiet. At first, I thought my life was ruined.

My mother saw my fierce face. She suggested I have a treasure hunt, but instead of looking for gold, I should look for baseball players. She promised to help by preparing a feast with all my favorite foods. I posted cardboard signs at the grocery store and the library. The signs said:

I'm looking for baseball players.
Come to 124 Willow Street
June 28 at 2:00 P.M.
FREE FOOD!

Do you think anyone showed up?

Your Turn!

 Need a Review? For additional help with homonyms, see page 165.

Ready to Try It? As you read other text, use what you've learned about homonyms to help you understand it.

Envision It! Words to Know

aqueducts

crouched

pillar

content
guidance
honor
thermal

Vocabulary Strategy for

⊙ Homographs

Context Clues Sometimes you may read a word you know, but the meaning doesn't make sense in the sentence. The word might be a homograph. Homographs are words that are spelled the same but have different pronunciations and meanings. For example, *lead* with a long e sound means to "go in front of," and *lead* with a short e sound means "a soft heavy metal."

1. If a word you know doesn't make sense in the sentence, it might be a homograph.

2. Look at the words around it. Can you figure out another meaning and pronunciation?

3. Try the new meaning in the sentence. Does it make sense?

Read "The Art of Architecture" on page 183. As you read, use context clues to find the meanings of homographs.

Words to Write Reread "The Art of Architecture." List the homographs and the other *Words to Know*, their pronunciations, including the syllables, and their meanings. Use a dictionary if needed. Then use those words to write a story about an ancient city.

THE ART OF ARCHITECTURE

The aqueducts of Paris, which are tunnels that carry water from one place to another, are an example of the ancient art of architecture. When Billy visited Paris with his grandmother, he crouched on his knees on the bank of the Seine to take a photograph of the famous structures, which were built centuries ago during Roman rule. Under his grandmother's guidance, Billy is learning more about architecture. Billy wants to be an architect when he grows up, which would honor the work of both his grandmother and grandfather who met in architecture school and designed many buildings in his hometown of Dallas. Ever since he could hold a crayon, he's been drawing houses with tall pillars and wide columns supporting giant roofs.

Now that Billy is older, he knows that architects do more than just draw fancy buildings. He feels a responsibility to conserve resources, and he has been reading about using thermal insulation to keep heating costs down. Even though he likes the idea of designing world-famous high rises, he knows that he will be happy and content with helping people make the best use of space and live better lives.

Your Turn!

 Need a Review?
For additional help with homographs, see page 164.

▶ **Ready to Try It?**
As you read other text, use what you've learned about homographs to help you understand it.

Related Words

Related words are words that have the same base word. *Sign*, *signal*, and *signature* are related because they all have the base word *sign*.

Sign

Signature

Signal

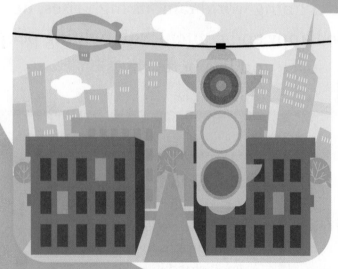

If you know the base words, you may be able to figure out the meanings of words related to it.

Compound Words

Compound words are words made of two smaller words. *Sandbox* and *ladybug* are compound words.

sand + **box** = **sandbox**

> Look for smaller words that *you* already know in unfamiliar words.

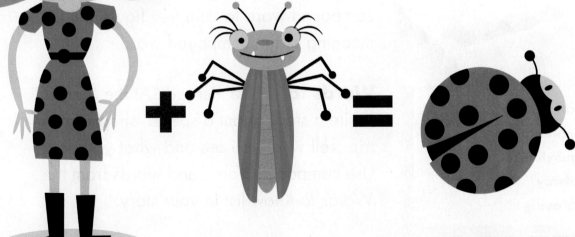

lady + **bug** = **ladybug**

Objectives
● Use word structure to figure out
words you don't know.

carpenter

carpetmaker

thread

knowledge
marketplace
merchant
plenty
straying

Vocabulary Strategy for

◉ Compound Words

Word Structure When you are reading,
you may come across a long word. Look
closely at the word. Do you see two small
words in it? It may be a compound word.
You may be able to use the two small words
to help you decode the meaning of the
compound word. For example, *goatseller*
is a person who sells goats.

1. Divide the compound word into its two
small words.

2. Think of the meaning of each small word
and put the two meanings together.

3. Try the new meaning in the sentence.
Does it make sense?

Read "At the Market" on page 187. Use
the meanings of the small words in each
compound word to help you figure out the
meaning of the compound word.

Words to Write Reread "At the Market."
Write a story about a special shopping
trip. Tell what you see and what you do.
Use compound words and words from the
Words to Know list in your story.

At the Market

Imagine a small town in Europe three hundred years ago. It is market day. People come from miles around to buy and sell things. They meet in the marketplace in the center of the town. Look, there is a farmer who has come to sell his fruits and vegetables. And here is another farmer who is selling chickens and geese. He has put them in wicker cages to keep them from straying. The carpenter has made chairs and tables for people's homes. The baker has baked plenty of homemade pies, cakes, and breads. This merchant sells things for sewing—cloth, needles, and thread. And over there is a carpetmaker. He has made beautiful carpets.

People walk from stall to stall looking at the items. They know what they are willing to pay, and they use this knowledge to decide what they will buy.

Is it different from today? Not really. Just think about your last trip to a modern marketplace—the shopping mall!

Your Turn!

❚❚ Need a Review? For additional help with compound words, see page 185.

▶ Ready to Try It? As you read other text, use what you've learned about compound words to help you understand it.

butterflies

collection

shoelaces

enormous

scattered

strain

Vocabulary Strategy for

🎯 Compound Words

Word Structure If you read a long word you don't know, look closely at it. Is it made up of two small words? If it is, then that long word is a compound word. You may be able to use the two small words to help you figure out the meaning of the compound word. For example, *praiseworthy* describes someone or something that is worthy of praise.

1. Divide the compound word into its two small words.

2. Think of the meaning of each small word, and put the two meanings together.

3. Try the new meaning in the context of the sentence to see if it makes sense.

Read "Get Organized" on page 189. Use the meanings of the small words in each compound word to help you figure out the meaning of the compound word.

Words to Write Reread "Get Organized." What do you collect? Write about your collection. Tell why you like to collect. Use words from the *Words to Know* list in your writing.

Get Organized

Are there enormous piles of stuff in your room? Are your things scattered everywhere? Is your closet clutter putting a strain on the door? Then it's time to take action!

First, realize that this will take time and work. Look at each thing. Ask yourself, "Do I use this? Will I ever use this?" For instance, you might need that extra button or pair of shoelaces sometime, but you'll probably never use that single sock with the big hole. So decide what to get rid of and what to keep. Think about the things you are getting rid of. Are they in good shape? Give them to a charity. If not, throw them out.

Next, put the things you are keeping into groups. Put each group together in one place. Put all the books on a shelf or table. Hang the clothes in the closet or put them in drawers. Do you have a collection of objects, such as rocks, postcards, butterflies, or stamps? Display them together on a shelf, table, or wall.

Now vacuum and dust your room. Congratulations! You have a shiny, clean, and well-organized room.

Your Turn!

Need a Review? For additional help with compound words, see page 185.

Ready to Try It? As you read other text, use what you've learned about compound words to help you understand it.

189

airport

delicious

raindrops

cellar

curious

described

farewell

homesick

memories

Vocabulary Strategy for

🔁 Compound Words

Word Structure You may come across a long word when you are reading. Look closely at it. Do you see two small words in it? Then it is a compound word. Use the two small words to figure out the meaning of the compound word. For example, a *classroom* is a room where a class is held.

1. Divide the compound word into its two small words.

2. Think of the meaning of each small word and then put the two meanings together. Does this help you understand the meaning of the compound word?

3. Try the new meaning in the context of the sentence. Does it make sense?

Read "How to Do a Move" on page 191. Use the two small words in each compound word to help you figure out its meaning.

Words to Write Reread "How to Do a Move." Write about what you think it would be like to move to a new place. Use words from the *Words to Know* list.

How to Do a Move

So you're moving. When you heard the news, did your stomach drop to the cellar? Did you become homesick before you had even left? Don't wait until you get to the airport to get ready for a move. Start planning now.

* Recognize that, just as raindrops are wet, you are going to be upset and unhappy. But that's OK. Just set a time limit. When the time is up, do something to make yourself feel better.

* Keep the memories. Take pictures of your old home, neighborhood, and friends. Make a scrapbook.

* Have a farewell party. Exchange addresses and telephone numbers with your friends.

* Be curious about your new town. Research the area at the library and on the Internet. It might be described in guidebooks. It might be known for a famous person or a delicious food. The more you know about the place, the more familiar it will feel when you get there.

Your Turn!

❚❚ Need a Review? For additional help with compound words, see page 185.

▶ Ready to Try It? As you read other text, use what you've learned about compound words to help you understand it.

Envision It! Genre

Fiction
fantasy
realistic fiction
historical fiction
fable
fairy tale
folk tale
legend
myth

Drama

Poetry

Informational Text
expository text
persuasive text
procedural text

Literary Nonfiction
autobiography
biography

Genre

As you read,
- decide if a selection is fiction or nonfiction.
- think about character, setting, plot, and theme.
- think about how the information in a selection is presented.

Literature is classified into different types, or genres. Knowing about genres can help you better understand what you read. It can also help you choose what to read when you read independently.

Ready to **Try** It?

Fiction describes imaginary events or people.

Genre	A **fantasy** is a story in which unbelievable things happen that can't happen in real life.	**Realistic fiction** is a made-up story that could really happen.	**Historical fiction** is a made-up story that takes place in the past.
Setting	The setting can be anytime or anywhere.	The setting is in a real place or in a place that seems real. The story may take place in the past or present.	The setting is a real place or like a real place. It has a specific focus on a time and place in history.
Characters	Characters have unreal qualities. Animals, toys, or objects may do things that only people can do in real life.	Human characters think, talk, and act like real people. Animals act like real animals.	Characters are like real people or based on real people. They fit in with the historical time and place.
Plot	The story can have any kind of conflict.	The plot is realistic and believable.	The story can have any kind of conflict, but it is often about a struggle in the world at the time, or a great accomplishment.

Genre	A **fable** is a short, imaginative story that has a lesson, or moral.	A **fairy tale** is a story about imaginary people or places from long ago.	A **folk tale** is a story or legend that is handed down from one generation to the next.
Setting	The setting can be anytime and anywhere.	The story usually takes place in an imagined place and at an imagined time. It may begin "Once upon a time in a land far away…"	Similar to a fairy tale, a folk tale usually takes place "long ago and far away."
Characters	Animals are often main characters. They can talk and act like humans.	Characters are usually "good" or "bad." They may be capable of superhuman actions or deeds.	The characters are flat, or simple. They may be capable of superhuman actions. They may be portrayed as "good" or "bad."
Plot	The plot, usually brief, is often about right versus wrong. The moral is usually stated at the end.	The story usually ends with the phrase "happily ever after."	The conflict is usually between two or more characters, or between characters and nature.

Fiction describes imaginary events or people.

Genre	A **legend** is a well-known story about exaggerated people or events.	A **myth** is a tale handed down by word of mouth. Myths are often told to explain human behavior or events in nature.
Setting	The story takes place in the past, but places are usually real.	The story is usually set in a fictional past. It begins "Long ago…" or "There once was…"
Characters	Characters are heroes with superhuman actions. They are often fictional versions of people in history.	Animals and things in nature, such as wind, can talk, think, and act like people.
Plot	The plot can be any conflict involving the hero character.	The plot is often a conflict between two or more characters, or between characters and nature.

Drama and **poetry** tell a real or fictional story in a unique way.

Genre	**Drama** tells a story that is meant to be performed.	**Poetry** is verse arranged in lines that have rhythm and may rhyme.
Features	Characters' dialogue and stage directions tell the story. There is information on characters and the setting.	Poetry has lines of text that are rhythmic. It has descriptive words and other poetic elements.
Organization	Drama is organized by lines of dialogue and stage directions.	A poem can have any organization. It may be organized in groups of lines called stanzas or in other patterns.
Includes. . .	plays; sketches; skits; scripts for radio or television	limericks; ballads; rhyming poems; shape poems

Informational text provides facts, details, and explanations.

	Expository text gives facts about real people, animals, places, and events.	Persuasive text tries to convince readers to think or do something.	Procedural text tells how to do something in clear, easy-to-understand steps.
Features	The information is factual. It may have headings, maps, indexes, time lines, and photos.	Persuasive text tells the author's point of view. There are persuasive words such as *must* and *should*.	The text has a list of necessary materials. There may be diagrams or illustrations with captions.
Organization	The text is often written in sequence. It may start off simply and build to harder information.	This is often written with a cause-and-effect or problem-solution pattern.	The text is usually chronological. It may be numbered in order of steps.
Includes...	book reports; articles; essays (cause-and-effect, compare-and-contrast, problem-solution)	editorials; letters to the editor; advertisements; some speeches	instructions or multi-step directions, such as recipes or rules for a game; how-to texts

Literary nonfiction is narrative text based on facts, real events, and real people.

Genre	An **autobiography** is the true story of a real person's life, written by that person.	A **biography** is the true story of a real person's life, written by another person.
Setting	The setting is a real place from the author's life.	The setting is a real place from the subject's life.
Characters	The characters are real people from real life.	The characters are real people from real life.
Plot	The conflict is often about a great accomplishment or about overcoming a great struggle.	The conflict is often about a great accomplishment or about overcoming a great struggle.

I Can Think About...

Fiction

realistic fiction

Is the story one that could really happen?

Is the setting real or a place that seems real?

Do the characters act like real people?

Is the plot realistic and believable?

folk tale

Has the story been handed down through generations?

Are the characters simple?

Are the characters either "good" or "bad"?

Does the story take place long ago and far away?

fantasy

Where does the story take place?

Do characters have unreal qualities?

Are the events in the story unbelievable?

What can I infer from the story's events?

fairy tale

Does the story take place in an imagined place?

Are the characters either "good" or "bad"?

Do characters have superhuman traits?

Does the story end happily?

myth

Does the story explain something about nature?

Are the first words "Long ago" or "There once was"?

Can animal characters talk, think, and act like people?

Is there a conflict between a character and nature?

historical fiction

Does the story take place in the past?

Is the story focused on a certain time and place in history?

Can I identify the characters' goals?

Is the story about a challenge in society?

legend

Does the story tell about a hero?

Does the story take place in the past?

Are characters' traits superhuman?

Are characters based on people in history?

fable

Where does the story take place?

Are the main characters animals?

Is the story about right versus wrong?

Is there a moral, or lesson?

201

I Can Think About...

Nonfiction

biography

Is this the true story of someone's life?

Are the characters real people from real life?

Is there a struggle or accomplishment?

autobiography

Is this the true story of someone's life?

Is this written by the person whose life it is about?

Are the characters real people from real life?

Is there a struggle or accomplishment?

procedural text

Are there steps that tell me what to do?

Is there a list of materials?

Are there diagrams, illustrations, or other graphics?

Is the text a recipe, a set of rules, or other instructions?

persuasive text

Does the text tell the author's point of view?

Are words such as *must* and *should* often used?

Is the text an editorial or advertisement?

expository text

Are there facts about real people, animals, places, and events?

Are there maps, time lines, or other graphics?

Are there captions or headings?

Does the text organization have a pattern?

I Can Think About...
Drama and Poetry

drama

Is the story meant to be performed?

Is there a description of the setting and a list of characters?

Are there lines of dialogue and stage directions?

Is this a stage play, a movie script, or skit?

poetry

Is this made up of words that have been put into lines?

Is there rhythm? Is there rhyme?

Can I identify a unique pattern in the organization?

Acknowledgments

Illustrations
135 Janet Stevens
154 Teresa Flavin
170 Wendell Minor

Photographs

Every effort has been made to secure permission and provide appropriate credit for photographic material. The publisher deeply regrets any omission and pledges to correct errors called to its attention in subsequent editions.

Unless otherwise acknowledged, all photographs are the property of Pearson Education, Inc.

Photo locators denoted as follows: Top (T), Center (C), Bottom (B), Left (L), Right (R), Background (Bkgd)

33 ©Tom Grill/Getty Images
34 (TL) ©Alan Schein Photography/Corbis
35 (TR) Getty Images
39 Brand X Pictures
41 (T, B) ©Royalty-Free/Corbis
47 Jupiter Images
49 ©Bartussek /Jupiter Images
57 (T) ©Charles O'Rear/Corbis
59 (BR) ©Royalty-Free/Corbis
65 Creasource/Corbis
67 Corbis
71 Art Wolfe/Stone/Getty Images
75 ©Richard T. Nowitz/Corbis
79 Digital Stock
80 (C) Charlie Schuck/Getty Images, (T) Dale Wilson/Getty Images, (B) Joe Sohm/Getty Images
81 (R, L) ©Bettmann/Corbis
89 ©Elvele Images Ltd/Alamy
91 (BL) ©Alan Schein Photography/Corbis, (BR) ©Bilderbuch/Design Pics/Corbis, (TL) ©Comstock Inc., (BR) ©Royalty-Free/Corbis
93 ©JM Labat/Photo Researchers, Inc.
99 Corbis
101 (B) ©Museum of History and Industry/ Library of Congress
107 (T, B) Getty Images

109 ©Accent Alaska/Alamy Images
120 (C) David A. Northcott/Corbis, (T) Getty Images, (B) Wesley Hitt/Alamy Images
121 (T) ©DK Images, (B) Getty Images
123 (T) ©Alain Dragesco-Joffe/Animals Animals/Earth Scenes, (B) ©Lex Hes/ABPL/ Animals Animals/Earth Scenes
126 (B) ©Roy Dabner/epa/Corbis, (C) Dennis Macdonald/PhotoLibrary Group, Ltd., (T) Jupiter Images
127 ©Stephen Wilkes/The Image Bank/Getty Images
128 (B) Corbis, (T) Massimo Borchi/Corbis, (C) vario images GmbH & Co.KG/Alamy Images
132 (C) A3W7WM/Alamy Images, (B) Richard Cummins/Corbis, (T) Robert Pickett/Corbis
133 (B) ©Volvox/Index Stock Imagery, Neil Fletcher/©DK Images
134 (C) ©David Frazier/Corbis, (T) ©Roger Bamber/Alamy Images, (B) Roy Morsch/ PhotoLibrary Group, Ltd.
136 (T) ©Philip Duff/Alamy Images, (B) Goolia Photography/Alamy, (C) Photolibrary
138 (C) Foodcollection/Alamy, (T) Getty Images, (B) VStock/Alamy
142 (B) ©DK Images, (C) G.Flayols/Corbis, (T) Patrice Thomas/Corbis
144 (B) ©James Marshall/Corbis, (T) Bill Stevenson/Alamy Images, (C) Radius Images / Jupiter Images
145 ©Richard Broadwell/Alamy Images
146 (C) DAVID NOBLE/Alamy Images, (B) Kai Wiechmann/Getty Images, (T) Taurus Taurus/PhotoLibrary Group, Ltd.
148 (B) Alamy, (C) Matt Cardy/Alamy Images, (T) PhotosIndia LLC/Alamy
152 (T) Ilan Rosen/Alamy Images, (B) Image99 /Jupiter Images, (C) Sue Flood/Getty Images
155 Creatas
156 (B) Corbis, (T) Foodfolio /PhotoLibrary Group, Ltd., (C) graficart/Alamy, (C) John-Patrick Morarescu/Photolibrary, (B) Photolibrary, (T) Will Stanton/Alamy Images
157 ©Randy Lincks/Corbis
158 (C) Alamy Images, (T) Greg Vaughn/ Alamy Images, (B) Nik Keevil/Alamy
160 (T) ©Yann Arthus-Bertrand/Corbis, (B) Anne-Marie Weber/Getty Images, (C) Mireille

205